The Right Ingredients

The **THANKFUL Method** for building
leaders people trust and follow

Dr. Andy Oguntola

The Right Ingredients

Copyright © 2026 by Dr. Andy Oguntola. All rights reserved.

www.AndyOguntola.com

Book Cover by: Zanae Oguntola

Paperback ISBN: 978-1-949562-38-5

First edition: 2026

Printed and bound in the United States of America.
Lakeland, Florida

Advance Praise For
The Right Ingredients

Great leaders lead with transparent hearts. The willingness to share personal experiences, both challenging and triumphant, is a vital component in developing not only effective leadership, but also a legacy that inspires others to follow. In *The Right Ingredients*: The **THANKFUL Method** for Building Leaders People Trust and Follow, Dr. Andy Oguntola demonstrates true courage by opening his life and sharing his journey as a husband, father, and community advocate. Through each trial and triumph, he has gained invaluable lessons that have shaped his passion, strengthened his resilience, and refined his approach to leadership. This book is the result of those experiences, a practical guide for anyone seeking to lead with purpose. Dr. Oguntola offers more than insight; he provides a blueprint for becoming the kind of leader people trust, respect, and willingly follow. If you are ready to lead and make a lasting impact, you will find that Dr. Oguntola truly has the right ingredients.

-Pastor Daniel E. Williams
The Family Church
Lake Wales, FL

As a CEO for more than 20 years at the same organization, this book served as a powerful reminder that leadership is a lifelong journey - one that requires continual learning, reflection, and intentional growth. From the first pages, I was drawn in by its genuine, transparent, and vulnerable approach to leadership. The **THANKFUL Method** speaks not only to seasoned leaders, but also to employees and emerging professionals who aspire to lead with trust and purpose at any stage of their career.

-Stacy Campbell-Domineck
President & CEO; Career Source Polk

This book is lovingly dedicated to my parents.

To my mother, who went home to be with the Lord on May 21, 2025. And to my father, who continues to walk this life with strength, faith, and quiet wisdom.

Everything I am as a leader began long before titles, degrees, or professional recognition. It began in our home, through the love, discipline, and example you both poured into me and my four sisters.

You taught us responsibility before recognition.
You taught us perseverance before praise.

And most importantly, you taught us that character matters more than comfort.

Mom: Some of my greatest memories with you were in the kitchen, not just preparing meals, but preparing me for life. You had a way of turning ordinary moments into lessons about integrity, kindness, and resilience. Even when I didn't fully understand it at the time, you were shaping the ingredients that would one day define the leader I would become.

You never allowed me to quit.
You never allowed me to settle.

And you constantly reminded me to become better than the generation before me.

Though you are no longer here to hold this book in your hands, your fingerprints are on every page. Your voice echoes in the values that guide this framework, and your spirit lives in the lessons that shaped the **THANKFUL Method**.

Dad: Your strength, consistency, and commitment to family showed me what faithfulness truly looks like. You modeled the quiet kind of leadership that doesn't seek applause, it simply shows up, day after day, doing what must be done.

Together, you gave us something far greater than opportunity. You gave us foundation.

This book exists because of the love you both invested, the standards you refused to lower, and the belief you had in us even when we doubted ourselves.

I carry your lessons with me into every room I lead, every person I mentor, and every table I am invited to serve.

Mom, this book is *for you*.
Dad, this book is *because of you*.

Thank you for the ingredients,
Your Son

Leadership is not built on charisma, position, or applause.
It is built in quiet kitchens, hard conversations, long prayers,
and ordinary moments where character is chosen over
comfort.

When the right ingredients are measured with humility,
faith, and consistency, a life of influence is formed.

Leadership, like a great meal, is never rushed.
It is prepared with care, served with love, and remembered
long after the table is cleared.

Dr. Andy Oguntola
Creator of the **THANKFUL** Method

Table of Contents

Foreword

Leadership is often measured by outcomes such as goals achieved, metrics reached, and milestones delivered. But the most enduring leadership is defined by something deeper: the impact we have on people, the environments we create, and the consistency with which we lead.

That is what makes *The Thankful Leadership Framework: From Preparation to Legacy* both timely and relevant.

I have had the privilege of working alongside Dr. Andy Oguntola at Florida Polytechnic University, where he serves as assistant vice president of enrollment management. In that role – and in every interaction – Dr. Oguntola brings a level of energy, authenticity, and commitment that is impossible to overlook. His passion is evident. His dedication is unwavering. And most importantly, his joy is contagious.

What truly sets Dr. Oguntola apart is not how he leads when things are going well, but how he leads in every circumstance, with integrity, conviction, and care.

This book reflects that experience in action.

The **THANKFUL Method** is not a theory developed in isolation. It is a practical framework shaped by experience, reflection, and a genuine commitment to leading people well. It offers a balanced approach that brings together accountability and empathy, discipline and adaptability, vision and execution.

One of the most compelling ideas in this book is that excellence in leadership is not accidental. It is built through daily choices, measured actions, and a disciplined commitment to growth. As Dr. Oguntola reinforces throughout these pages, effective leadership is not defined by a single moment or trait, but by the consistency and care we bring to how we lead others.

That principle is especially relevant in today's environment, where preparing the next generation requires more than technical expertise. It calls for leaders who are thoughtful, grounded, and deliberate in how they develop people. The framework outlined in this book offers a clear and practical guide, equipping leaders to create cultures where individuals are supported, challenged, and positioned to succeed.

This is not a book to read just once and set aside. It is one you return to at every stage of your leadership journey, applying its lessons, refining your approach, and strengthening your legacy.

I am confident this book will inspire and guide leaders for many years to come.

- Dr. Devin Stephenson
President; Florida Polytechnic University

Letter To The Reader

Before we begin this journey together, I want to thank you. In a world filled with countless books, voices, and perspectives, you chose to open these pages. That choice alone tells me something important about you, you care about growth, about leadership, and about becoming better than you were yesterday.

This book was not written in a moment. It was formed over a lifetime.

It was shaped in conversations with mentors, in moments of failure that forced reflection, in leadership opportunities that stretched my character, and most importantly, in the quiet lessons passed down from my parents. Long before I understood leadership theories or organizational strategy, I was learning something far more powerful at home: the value of discipline, humility, love, faith, and responsibility.

Some of my earliest memories were not in boardrooms or classrooms, but in the kitchen. Watching meals come together ingredient by ingredient taught me something I would not fully understand until much later in life, great outcomes rarely happen by accident. They are the result of intentional preparation.

Leadership works the same way. Just like a great meal requires the right ingredients measured with care, leadership requires the right qualities developed with patience. Character must be cultivated. Integrity must be practiced. Humility must be chosen. And growth must be pursued even when it is uncomfortable.

This book introduces a framework that I have come to call The **THANKFUL Method**, a set of leadership ingredients that, when practiced consistently, create leaders who elevate others rather than simply manage them.

But this book is not just about leadership in organizations. It is about leadership in life. It is about the choices we make when no one is watching. The standards we hold ourselves to when the path becomes difficult.

The way we influence our families, our communities, and the people who trust us to guide them forward.

My hope is that as you move through these pages, you will not simply read ideas, you will reflect on your own ingredients. Which qualities are already strong? Which ones need refinement? Which ones have yet to be added to the recipe of your leadership?

Because the truth is this: Leadership is not reserved for titles. It is prepared daily by the decisions we make.

If these pages challenge you to grow, encourage you during difficulty, or inspire you to lead with greater purpose, then this book has fulfilled its mission.

Thank you for taking this journey with me. Now let's step into the kitchen and begin preparing the right ingredients.

With gratitude,
- Dr. Andy Oguntola

Preface

Leadership is often presented as something you master through titles, training, or time. I have learned that leadership is none of those things. Instead, this characteristic is formed through pressure, discernment, and a willingness to be shaped by moments you did not ask for but were entrusted with anyway.

Over the years, I have had the privilege of leading in spaces where decisions carried tremendous weight. People were impacted. Families were affected. Outcomes mattered. In those moments, I recognized the fact that leadership could not be sustained by instinct alone. Talent was not enough. Passion was not enough. Even experience, on its own, was not enough. What was required was a consistent posture, a framework that could guide decisions when clarity was limited, and pressure was high.

Through my journey of leadership, reflection, faith, and discernment, I have developed what I now call the **THANKFUL Method**. This framework was not created in theory or borrowed from a single model. It was shaped over time through my personal leadership experiences, moments of success, instances of failure, seasons of growth, and times of correction. Each **THANKFUL** principle emerged when I paid attention to what factors strengthened teams and which ones quietly weakened them.

I see these principles as being:

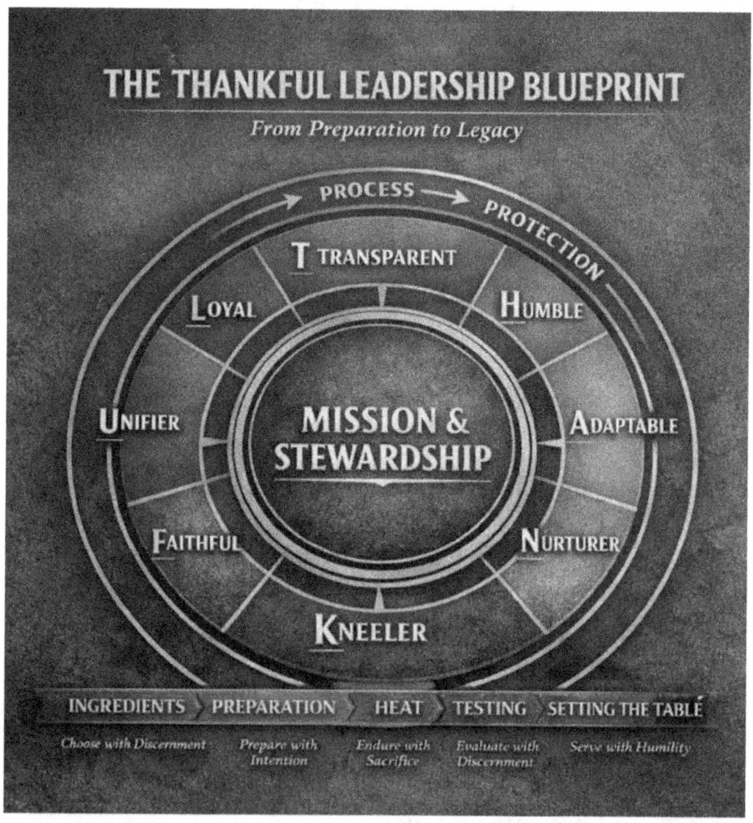

I believe deeply that these leadership qualities must present as well as translate effectively in every environment. It must work in boardrooms and break rooms, in churches and classrooms, in organizations and in homes. The **THANKFUL Method** is rooted in that belief. It is not dependent on industry, title, or personality for it to be

16

effective. It is rooted in values that hold under pressure and principles that remain steady when circumstances change.

To guide us in our discussion, I use meal prep, cooking, and my kitchen as metaphors for leadership. Why? Because leadership, like every great meal, is built through preparation, patience, and intention. Every ingredient matters. Timing matters. Discernment matters. And when one element is off, the entire outcome is affected.

Leadership is no different.

As you read this book, you have a chance to reflect honestly on your own impact. I would like to invite you to evaluate your own leadership pantry. Now is your time to pause and determine what is fresh, what needs attention, and what may no longer belong. You have an opportunity to uplevel your influence, whether you are leading a team, a family, an organization, or even just yourself. I believe these principles will help you to lead with clarity, humility, and purpose.

Your journey is not about perfection. It is about stewardship. Leadership is about becoming intentional with the influence you have been given and understanding the responsibility that comes with it. This will always involve risk, sacrifice, and growth. But when approached with discernment and faith, it can also be one of the most meaningful callings you will ever accept.

Before The Ingredients Come Together

Leadership is one of the most talked-about subjects in the world yet, it is also one of the most misunderstood concepts. It is praised, pursued, and positioned as the solution to nearly every organizational challenge. We promote it, demand it, and critique it relentlessly. Still, if we are honest, many of us quietly struggle behind the scenes, unsure why our influence feels heavier than it should and why results come at such a personal toll.

This struggle exists because leadership is often spoken of as a position instead of a posture, an outcome instead of a process, and visibility instead of responsibility. We celebrate results while overlooking the cost required to sustain them. Strategy gets the spotlight. Sacrifice happens in the shadows. I simply want to explore that honest side of us and open up dialogue on both the struggle within leadership and how to lighten the load.

I have not written from a place of perfection, but from experience, wins and wounds, confidence and collapse. I have served in leadership long enough to know that titles do not make leaders, charisma does not sustain leaders, and good intentions do not protect leaders from burnout, broken relationships, or regret.

Too many leadership conversations focus on strategy without acknowledging the sacrifice required. But we can't solely focus on performance without talking about presence. We also can't aim for success without embracing sustainability. How unfortunate it would be to celebrate outcomes while neglecting the people, families, and faith that make those outcomes possible.

Leadership, like a great meal, is never accidental. What you bring into it matters. Likewise, what you leave out matters just as much.

Therefore, I would like to invite you to answer a different question: *Do you have the right ingredients to lead well and live whole?*

The chapters that follow are your chance to find out. In the process, my aim is to support leaders in building cultures that last without losing themselves in the process.

Welcome to the kitchen

Who's In The Kitchen

Some of the most memorable meals in life are never about the food. They are about the people standing nearby, the ones who stayed late, cleaned up quietly, and made sure everyone else was fed before themselves. The truth is, no great meal is ever created alone. Behind every finished plate is a kitchen full of unseen hands.

My favorite kitchen is the one filled with my family.

There were seasons when leadership asked more of me than it should have. Times when my energy was spent on others, and the people I loved most received what was left. Yet my family stayed. They believed. They made space for growth even when it was inconvenient. They extended grace when I was tired, distracted, or stretched too thin.

My wife has been the steady presence behind every chapter of my life. When my confidence wavered, hers did not. When the weight felt heavy, she carried it with quiet strength.

She supported the calling even when it disrupted our routines, our time, and our comfort. She believed in what this work could become long before it ever took shape. Her love has been patient, her counsel honest, and her commitment unwavering. I would not be the leader I am, or the man I strive to be, without her.

My children are my greatest teachers. They remind me that leadership is not measured by applause or accomplishment, but by presence.

They see me without titles, without platforms, and without performance. They have waited when meetings ran long. They have celebrated small moments with me when they could have asked for more. They are the reason I care so deeply about doing leadership the right way. Because success that costs your family is never success at all.

Everything I know about excellence began at home. In the way love was shown when words were unnecessary. In the grace extended when mistakes were made. In the quiet encouragement that said, "Keep going," even when the path felt uncertain.

This book may carry my name, but it holds their fingerprints on every page.

Therefore, before the ingredients come together and before the meal is prepared and served, I want to say this with clarity and gratitude:

To my wife: *Thank you for believing in me when I struggled to believe in myself.*

To my children: *Thank you for sharing me, supporting me, and reminding me what truly matters.*

To my mother and father: *Thank you for every moment you gave me.*

You are the reason I stayed in the kitchen long enough to finish preparing the meal.

And for that, I am ***forever thankful***.

Start From Scratch

Growing up, I remember standing in the kitchen and watching my mother cook. She would move with confidence and care, never rushed, always intentional. "Son," she would say, "you need to pay attention and watch how I prepare these meals." Every dish was different. Every flavor was distinct. And somehow, no matter how simple the ingredients, the food always carried a taste only a mother could provide.

Stuffed Peppers, Baked Chicken and Rice, or traditional dishes of hers, all were works of art, cooked to perfection. My dad, sisters, and I all savored each meal.

Every time I watched her cook, she would tell me what to grab, where to find it in the pantry, and when to wait. Some meals required patience. Others required precision. None of them was accidental. At the time, I thought she was simply teaching me how to cook. What I did not realize was that she was teaching me how to lead.

My time with her in the kitchen was never just about food. It was about preparation. She was modeling responsibility, awareness, and care. She was showing me how to be attentive to detail and to respect the process. More than that, she was quietly building something in me she knew I would need one day, the ability to stand on my own when she was no longer there to guide me.

Looking back now, I understand that leadership begins long before we ever carry a title. It sprouts in the small moments where someone takes the time to pour into us, nurture us, and prepare us for a future we cannot yet see.

My mother was not just feeding her family. She was forming a leader.

And in her absence, the lessons she left behind would continue to guide me.

Starting from scratch is often the most important step in leadership, and it's one we should never be afraid to take. Too often, we try to build something new while holding on to pieces of the past that no longer serve us.

Imagine preparing a meal with fresh ingredients laid out neatly across your kitchen counter. Everything is ready. The recipe is clear. Then, just before you begin, you grab one last thing from the refrigerator and notice leftovers that have been sitting there for a couple of days. You pause and consider adding them to the new meal you're about to cook.

Chances are, you wouldn't do that. You would either reheat the leftovers and eat them as they are or throw them away and commit to creating something new. You wouldn't mix yesterday's leftovers into a fresh dish and expect the result to be excellent.

Leadership works the same way.

There are absolutely lessons from our past worth keeping. But there are also habits, mindsets, and behaviors that must be discarded. When it comes to leadership, you eat the meat and spit out the bones. Take what is good. Learn from what is valuable. But don't reuse past tactics simply because they are familiar.

Every experience, good or bad, served its purpose in the moment. Some teach you what to repeat. Others inform you of what to never do again. Not everything from your past belongs in your future. Growth often requires courage to let go.

Leadership is not easy to define. Nearly everyone has been affected by how someone has led (or attempted to lead) them, yet very few truly understand how to incorporate it into their life. Leadership is discussed in books, debated in classrooms, promoted in boardrooms, and demanded in workplaces across every industry. Scholars attempt to define it through theory. Mentors attempt to demonstrate it through experience. Supervisors often measure it through outcomes. And yet, despite so much chatter, leadership remains one of the most misunderstood and misapplied concepts in modern organizations.

Too often, leadership is reduced to authority, position, or charisma. Leadership, however, is far more human than that.

It is influence before it is instruction. Responsibility before recognition. Sacrifice before success.

Strong leadership is shaped by context, tested through adversity, and refined through self-awareness. It is not static.

It evolves as people evolve. It must be paired with a willingness to learn, unlearn, and relearn.

So why is something we ascribe to so difficult to attain?

The challenge is that many people step into leadership believing they must already have the answers. They feel pressure to perform, to project confidence, and to avoid showing uncertainty. Yet true leadership rarely begins with answers. It begins with the courage to ask better questions.

After seventeen years of serving in various leadership roles, if I could speak to my younger self, my advice would be simple:

Forget everything you think you know and begin again. Start from scratch.

Too often, we step into new roles carrying old assumptions. We bring habits that worked in previous seasons. We borrow styles that have served others well. We rely on tools that once felt effective but no longer fit the environment we are in.

The world is changing rapidly. Culture, technology, methodology, and workflows seem to shift almost daily. What worked five years ago may be ineffective today. What succeeded under one leader may fail under another. Leadership does not exist in a vacuum. It is shaped by time, people, culture, and circumstance. And each of these things is evolving at light speed all around us.

Because of this, at some point, every leader encounters a defining moment, an experience that reshapes how they see themselves and the world around them. That moment rarely arrives through success. More often, it arrives through struggle.

For me, it came at 17.

At 17, I was working two jobs while still in school. After sports practice each afternoon, I would head straight to a pizza shop. There, I put on a mascot costume, stood on a street corner, and flipped a sign advertising hot and ready pizza. Cars passed by, sometimes honking in laughter. After long stretches in that hot, uncomfortable suit, I would go inside, wash my hands, and work in the kitchen making pizzas until closing.

On weekends, I opened the pizza shop and prepared for the first shift. Once the mid-shift arrived, I would then drive thirty minutes to an amusement park to work as a cook. One day in particular stands out vividly. The park was packed. Customers waited in a line that stretched down the block. Inside the kitchen, the pace was relentless. I was dropping fish, chicken strips, and fries into hot grease repeatedly. Sweat filled the air. Fatigue settled in. The ticket machine never stopped printing orders.

Then an unusually large ticket emerged. It included nearly every item on the menu. For a moment, the kitchen went quiet. We all stared at the receipt, silently acknowledging the challenge ahead. Then we got to work, accepting the task.

I ran to grab more boxes of chicken and fish. Fresh fries were dropped. Pressure mounted. Frustration grew. It felt like everyone wanted to quit. When we finally sent the trays out, there was a brief sense of accomplishment.

We did it! But then, out of curiosity, I looked closely at the receipt.

That was the moment everything changed.

A single family had ordered fifteen chicken baskets, each priced at $9.50. As I did the math, my heart sank. At that time, I was earning $8.15 an hour. Standing there, exhausted and covered in sweat, I realized my labor for an entire hour was worth less than a single chicken basket. I finally understood the meaning of value.

Disheartened, it felt as though my worth had been reduced to a handful of fries and a few strips of chicken.

I remember the feeling clearly.

Shock. Confusion. A deep, unsettling realization. I knew life had more to offer me than what that moment suggested. I made a promise to myself that day. I would not remain in a place where my value felt so small. I would never allow myself to feel that way again.

Leadership was not something I understood at seventeen. I did not know how to articulate frameworks. But that day, in the middle of exhaustion and adversity, the foundation of a leader was formed within me.

Since that moment, I have come to see that what separates leaders is not the absence of hardship, but what we choose to do with it. Hard moments either harden you or shape you. They either shrink your vision or clarify it.

Sometimes things must fall apart before they can fall into place. Leadership requires humility, the willingness to stumble, to fail, and to reflect.

Falling on your face teaches you the pace of progress and the cost of growth.

Just like preparing an exceptional meal, leadership and team building are deliberate processes. A great meal depends on the quality of its ingredients. Nothing is left to chance. Each component is selected with care. If something is missing, the cook searches until it is found, knowing that one missing ingredient can alter the entire experience.

Therefore, my first advice to you, as you begin this journey, is simple: know what you're working with.

Before you rush to change systems, set new goals, or cast a bigger vision, pause long enough to take inventory. Survey your team honestly. Look beyond titles and résumés. Pay attention to how people show up when the pressure is low and when it rises. Scout not just for talent, but for teachability, character, and hunger, the kind of qualities that don't always show up on paper but always reveal themselves over time.

Too many leaders assume they know their ingredients, only to discover later that something essential was missing all along. This is your moment to slow down and look closely.

Finding the right ingredient mix is revealed not only through vision but through discernment. The ability to recognize potential, character, and alignment separates average leadership from great leadership. When leaders take time to find the right people, they move beyond filling roles and begin building something meaningful.

When the right individuals come together, everything shifts. Performance improves. Communication strengthens. Trust deepens. Teams move from functioning to flourishing. What once felt heavy becomes energizing. The impossible shifts to become achievable.

This transformation is never accidental. It is the result of intentional leadership and thoughtful selection of people who share purpose, values, and commitment.

This is where synergy is created. It is never forced through slogans or meetings. Instead, it emerges naturally when people are aligned. When the right ingredients are present, the result exceeds expectations. Average becomes great. Effort turns into excellence.

Before we go further, I would like to invite you to pause and look inward.

Let's determine what fresh ingredients you need and where you may need to start from scratch.

- Are there any assumptions you have been carrying that no longer serve you?
- What habits do you rely on without questioning?
- What beliefs about yourself and others may need to be released?
- What fresh ingredients do you need to bring to the kitchen?

Starting from scratch is not an admission of failure. It is an act of courage. It is the willingness to clear the counter, examine the ingredients, and prepare something better than before.

Leadership does not begin with control. It begins with awareness. And awareness always starts within. Before we can lead well, we must first be honest about what we're carrying with us, and whether it still belongs in the kitchen we're trying to build.

Chapter 1 Reflection

- What leadership assumptions am I carrying that may no longer serve me?
- Where did I learn how to lead, and who shaped that example?
- When was the first moment I realized I wanted more from my journey of leadership?
- What would it look like for me to truly start from scratch?

The Proper Ingredients

Starting from scratch creates space, but that is not all. It also creates exposure. When the counter is cleared and the noise is removed, leaders are left with a quiet and often uncomfortable realization. Intention alone is not enough. Desire does not equal direction. Passion does not guarantee progress. What ultimately determines the outcome is what we choose to bring into the process.

So where do we begin? We must start with the proper ingredients.

Leadership without a framework is like walking into a grocery store without a list. You may grab what looks good, what is familiar, or what you have always used before. Some meals turn out fine. Others disappoint. The inconsistency is not because you lacked effort. It is because you lacked intention.

Leaders without a framework rely heavily on instinct. Leaders with a framework lead with clarity.

Therefore, I want to share a framework that has forever changed my approach to leadership. This framework did not emerge quickly or casually. It was formed over years of observation, failure, prayer, and refinement in my own leadership environments. As I paid attention to the characteristic which helped me to become a stronger leader, I noticed patterns. In my searching to find what worked best, I realized that I constantly wondered why some leaders sustained impact while others quietly burned out. I had watched teams thrive under certain leaders and fracture under others, despite the fact that both individuals appeared equally talented. What separated them was not charisma or volume. Instead, I discovered that it all came down to grounding.

Leaders who endured were steady. They understood balance, alignment, and stewardship. Drawing from lived lessons and from everything they taught me, a framework took shape, one that became the core of this book.

You might wonder: Why do we even need a framework? While there may not be a clear reason at first, the differences between leaders who use a framework and those who do not become clear over time. Leaders without a framework react to pressure. They chase urgency. They solve problems in isolation. Leaders with a framework respond with clarity. They lead with consistency. They build trust intentionally.

**One group manages chaos.
The other cultivates culture.**

Leadership success is never accidental. It is built, measured, and sustained with purpose. Therefore, we need benchmarks. Just as no single ingredient can carry an entire recipe, no single leadership trait can carry an organization. Talent alone is insufficient. Vision without care creates burnout. Compassion without accountability creates confusion. Leadership breaks down when one ingredient attempts to do the work of all the others.

Through experience and reflection, I developed the **THANKFUL Method**. To me, this was always more than a checklist. Instead, it has become a way of being. I see it as less of a rigid system and more as a living framework. It represents the essential ingredients required for moving teams from survival to excellence. When practiced consistently, it creates environments where people feel valued, challenged, protected, and inspired.

Nothing about the **THANKFUL Method** is hierarchical. Each ingredient matters equally. When one is missing, the entire dish suffers. When one is overused, balance is lost. And as we continue in our leadership journey, we must learn how to use each one.

Here are the leadership ingredients that have built the foundation of my framework and instilled the **THANKFUL Method** into my everyday habits.

It starts with being **THANKFUL**, which means to be:

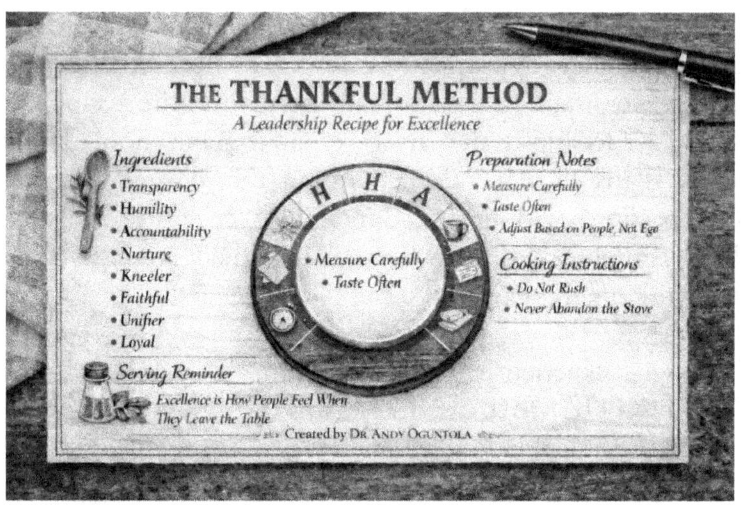

Transparent

Transparency is the foundation of trust. Teams do not expect perfection from their leaders, but they do expect honesty. Transparency means communicating clearly, directly, and consistently. It means uttering what needs to be said without hidden agendas or manufactured responses.

True transparency aligns words and behavior. Leaders cannot say they care while remaining absent. They cannot promote openness while avoiding hard conversations. Transparency requires presence. Leaders who have never worked openly with their teams will struggle to earn credibility.

**Transparency is not weakness.
It is courage practiced daily.**

A transparent leader does not hide behind email when a conversation is needed. They do not shift narratives to preserve control. They do not promise what they cannot deliver. Transparency requires presence. It requires courage. It requires the willingness to have difficult conversations face-to-face and heart-to-heart.

Think of transparency as cooking with the lights on. Nothing is hidden in the back kitchen. Every ingredient is visible. Every step is accountable. When leaders operate in the light, trust grows naturally. When they operate in the shadows, suspicion grows quietly.

Transparency is not weakness. It is strength under exposure. It is integrity practiced daily.

Humble

Humility separates effective leaders from positional leaders. Humility is not thinking less of yourself but thinking of yourself less. It is the willingness to absorb pressure without deflecting blame. It consistently chooses service over spotlight.

Team members deserve leaders who do not allow titles, education, or income to elevate themselves above others. Authority never equals superiority. Humble leaders let their work speak for itself. They invite collaboration and ownership. After all, I have discovered that ego creates distance, but humility builds trust.

Picture humility as seasoning. Too much ego overpowers the entire dish. But when humility is present in the right measure, everything else comes alive. Conversations become safer. Collaboration becomes stronger. Innovation becomes freer.

And the leader who kneels low enough will always see farther than the one standing tall on pride.

Adaptable

For leadership to remain dynamic, it must be adaptable. What worked yesterday may fail today. Therefore, an openness to a shift in a new direction is key. Adaptability is the ability to pivot without losing purpose. It responds thoughtfully rather than reacts emotionally.

Adaptable leaders read the room. They assess context. They adjust strategies without abandoning values. In moments of flux, adaptability becomes the bridge between chaos and clarity.

In the kitchen, if the heat is too high, you adjust the flame. If an ingredient runs out, you modify the recipe without abandoning the meal. You do not throw everything away because one element changed.

Adaptability is that adjustment. It is the quiet confidence that says, "We may alter the method, but we will not abandon the mission."

In moments of flux, adaptability becomes the bridge between chaos and clarity.

Nurturer

Many leaders assume teams should arrive fully formed and ready to perform. Reality, however, is quick to tell us otherwise. People are complex. Growth requires cultivation.

Nurturing leadership invests time, patience, and intention into development. It corrects with care. It challenges mindset while still offering support. Nurturing builds a level of connection that people do not want to break. It transforms workplaces into communities.

Think of a gardener. The soil must be prepared. The seed must be protected. Watering must be consistent. Sunlight must be steady. Growth is rarely dramatic, but it is always intentional.

As I often say, work is easy. Working alongside people is what is hard. That is why nurturing matters.

When people feel developed rather than used, they stay. When they feel seen rather than managed, they grow. And when they grow, the entire culture strengthens.

Therefore, nurture transforms workplaces into communities.

Kneeler

This ingredient is deeply personal to me. A kneeler is a leader who understands the power of prayer. These individuals know that prayer is not a last resort. Instead, it is a leadership discipline.

In the kitchen of leadership, kneeling is the pause before the preparation. It is the quiet moment before the noise. It is the surrender that says, "I am responsible, but I am not ultimate."

A kneeling leader seeks guidance in moments of clarity and confusion. They pray for their teams, their families, and their decisions. This posture keeps leaders grounded and aligned with a purpose greater than themselves. If prayer has no place in your leadership, this framework may challenge you. It challenged me too. But it changed everything when I welcomed Divine guidance into my leadership and began to seek help each time, I needed it.

Faithful

Faithfulness begins at home. Faithfulness is stamina. It is the ability to stay present, committed, and engaged long after the initial enthusiasm fades. It means choosing consistency over convenience, especially when no one is watching and no applause is coming.

Leadership demands endurance. Faithful leaders do not disappear when the work becomes repetitive, relationally heavy, or emotionally draining. They stay. They show up. They remain steady in how they lead, even when progress is slow or recognition is absent.

I pay close attention to how leaders treat their families, not to judge them, but because it reveals something foundational. How someone gives their time, attention, and patience at home is often how they will eventually lead others. If a leader cannot be faithful to the people they love most, it becomes difficult to believe they will show faithfulness to the people they lead professionally.

Faithfulness at home looks like presence when work could easily interrupt. It looks like patience when exhaustion sets in. It looks like choosing to engage instead of retreat, to listen instead of multitasking, and to stay emotionally available even when the day has taken more than expected.

In the kitchen, faithfulness looks like staying with the dish until it is done. You don't walk away halfway through and expect a great meal. You don't rush the process just because it takes longer than you planned. Heat must be managed. Timing must be honored. Attention must be sustained. The cook who abandons the stove too early doesn't ruin the meal because of bad intentions, but because of absence.

Leadership works the same way.

Leaders who lack faithfulness often begin well. They are passionate, driven, and inspiring at the start. But when results take longer, when people need more care than expected, or when leadership becomes inconvenient, they drift. They show up inconsistently. Their commitment wavers. Teams feel it immediately.

Children do not need perfect parents. Teams do not need flawless leaders. Both need presence. Both need consistency. Both need to know that the person responsible for them will not disappear when things get hard.

If you cannot sustain attention, patience, and care with your family, where love already exists, it becomes nearly impossible to offer those same qualities to employees who are watching, evaluating, and deciding whether or not you can be trusted.

Faithfulness builds trust slowly and quietly. It is formed in daily decisions to stay, to listen, to finish what you started.

Over time, it creates safety. And safety allows people, at home and at work, to grow.

Faithful leadership is not loud. It does not demand recognition. It simply shows up again tomorrow.

That kind of faithfulness changes families.
That kind of faithfulness sustains teams.
That kind of faithfulness is an ingredient no leader can afford to leave out.

Unifier

Unity is easy when things are going well. Yet true leadership is revealed during conflict. A unifier does not avoid tension. They address issues that stand in the way with clarity and compassion.

A unifier listens before labeling. They seek understanding before issuing judgment. They do not weaponize information or take sides to preserve popularity. Instead, they stand in the middle and build bridges where walls have begun to form.

Think of a unifier as the binding agent in a recipe. Flour, sugar, butter, and eggs sitting separately accomplish nothing. But an ingredient that binds them together that creates structure. Without it, everything crumbles under pressure.

In teams, personalities differ. Perspectives clash. Expectations collide. The unifier does not force sameness. They align differences toward shared purpose. They remind the team of the mission when emotions threaten to redirect focus.

Unifiers bring people together when trust is fractured. They guide teams toward resolution rather than assigning blame. Unity is not accidental. It is built through intentional leadership.

Loyal

Loyalty is not demanded. It is always earned. When a leader asks for loyalty to be pledged, it is an indicator that they often lack it themselves.

Loyalty is more than a popularity contest. Instead, it is demonstrated through protection, consistency, and respect for the mission and the people. Loyalty rooted in self-interest collapses quickly. Loyalty rooted in purpose sustains teams through difficulty. Loyalty shifts when promotions are offered or recognition fades. But loyalty rooted in shared purpose sustains teams through difficulty.

Imagine loyalty as the steady flame beneath the stove. It does not flicker wildly when the kitchen becomes busy. It remains constant, providing the consistent heat needed to finish the meal. When that flame disappears, everything cools quickly.

Loyal leaders speak well of their teams when they are absent. They honor commitments. They refuse to exploit people for temporary gain. They understand that loyalty is not blind allegiance; it is faithful alignment with a greater mission.

When leaders are loyal to their values, their people, and their calling, teams feel safe. And when people feel safe, they give their best.

Loyalty is not about control. It is about a covenant.

THE THANKFUL LEADERSHIP BLUEPRINT

From Preparation lo Legocy

Now that we have looked at the ingredients, it is key to remember that something special happens when you blend them. Leave one out, and the dish is ruined. Transparency without humility becomes arrogance. Faithfulness without adaptability becomes rigidity. Loyalty without unity becomes blind allegiance. The power of the **THANKFUL Method** is found in an appropriate balance that uses the right mix in each unique situation.

When leaders commit to this framework, teams feel it. Communication strengthens. Trust deepens. Accountability becomes healthier. People show up not because they must, but because they want to.

Organizations struggle not from lack of talent, but from lack of alignment. The **THANKFUL Method** provides a shared language and standard. It offers leaders a mirror and a road map.

I have come to see that Leadership is built daily through my choices, conversations, and character. The proper ingredients matter. Each of us has a chance to be intentional about what we bring into the mix. As we do, we get to create cultures that last, discover results that matter, and leave legacies that extend far beyond our titles.

The THANKFUL Leadership Assessment Tool

Curious how well you live out the **THANKFUL Method**? I would like to invite you to pause and honestly rate how you display each ingredient on a scale of 1 to 5.

For this exercise, 1 indicates that this attribute is rarely demonstrated, and 5 indicates that it is consistently demonstrated.

Transparent: I communicate honestly, clearly, and consistently, and my actions align with my words.

____

Humble: I lead without ego, value all team members equally, and allow my work to speak for itself.

____

Adaptable: I respond effectively to change and make thoughtful decisions under pressure.

____

Nurturer: I intentionally invest in my team member's growth, development, and well-being.

____

Kneeler: I seek guidance through prayer and lead with spiritual grounding and humility.

____

Faithful: I demonstrate commitment to my family, my team, and the mission I have been entrusted with through consistent action.

____

Unifier: I address conflict directly and work to restore harmony and trust within the team.

____

Loyal: I model loyalty through protection, advocacy, and respect for the mission and the people.

____

Total: _____________

Your score is not your identity. Instead, it simply reveals strengths, gaps, and opportunities for growth. The goal is not perfection, but progress.

Reflection Questions for Leaders

1. Which ingredient of the **THANKFUL Method** comes most naturally to me, and why?
2. Which ingredient do I tend to avoid or neglect under pressure?
3. How does my leadership style impact the emotional and psychological safety of my team?
4. What would change in my immediate sphere of influence if I consistently practiced this method every day?
5. What is one intentional action I can take this week to strengthen one ingredient?

High Level Of Excellence

Over the years, I have observed two very different kinds of leaders. Some are exceptional with details. They can thrive in the weeds. They fine-tune processes, track metrics, and ensure every small piece is in its proper place. Others lead from a higher altitude. Their vision is expansive. Creativity flows freely. Innovation feels effortless. Both types of leaders are talented. Both bring value. Yet too often, they struggle to work together.

Imagine walking into a kitchen where two cooks are preparing a meal. One walks in holding a beautifully written recipe. He understands the final outcome. He knows what the dish should taste like, how it should look when plated, and the experience it should create for the people sitting at the table.

The other cook walks in carrying the ingredients. Fresh vegetables, carefully selected spices, measured portions, and the tools needed to prepare the meal. Individually, both bring something valuable. But neither can produce the meal alone.

A recipe without ingredients remains an idea. Ingredients without a recipe become confusion. Only when both come together does the meal finally begin to take shape.

Leadership works the same way.

Some leaders naturally carry the recipe. They see the vision, the direction, and the future possibilities.

Others bring the ingredients. They focus on the details, the systems, and the steps required to bring the vision to life.

Excellence happens when both leaders realize they were never meant to compete for control of the kitchen. They were meant to cook together.

The disconnect happens because each group fails to appreciate what the other provides. Detail-driven leaders can become so focused on precision that they lose sight of possibility. Visionary leaders can soar so high that they overlook the importance of daily operations. One fears losing control. The other fears being constrained. In time, both become frustrated with the other, not because of a lack of skill, but because they lack balance in their strengths.

I have seen leaders be so consumed by details that they become afraid of their own potential. Their precision turns into paralysis, and they become afraid of heights. Before they know it, their structure becomes a ceiling. On the other hand, I have seen leaders enamored with innovation to the point that they dismiss the discipline required to execute a single idea. I think we all can agree that vision without preparation eventually collapses under its own weight.

But what if our blending of ingredients requires us to adopt both detail-oriented preparation and creative vision casting?

Transformation is not loss; it is purpose fulfilled. Ingredients were never meant to remain untouched. They were created to blend together into something greater than they were on their own.

When leaders commit to such a balance, something powerful happens. Details no longer compete with vision; they support it. Creativity no longer feels reckless; it becomes intentional. Excellence begins to form quietly, long before anyone sees the finished product.

There is no better feeling than walking into a home and immediately smelling a meal already in progress. Even if you have not seen the food yet, the aroma tells you everything you need to know. Care was taken. Time was invested. Someone stayed in the kitchen long enough to get it right. That is what a high level of excellence produces: an atmosphere people want to enter and remain in.

When we balance our levels of detail and vision, we can create the same effect. Before results are visible, the culture already feels different. Trust grows. Engagement increases. People lean in rather than pull away. Together, let's learn how to create that aroma through awareness, balance, and intentional preparation.

Knowing what ingredients you need does not guarantee you can cook a great meal. Anyone can stock a pantry. Excellence is revealed in how those ingredients are measured, handled, and applied. This is where many leaders stumble.

They care deeply. They work hard. Their intentions are good. Yet results feel inconsistent. Morale fluctuates. Trust feels fragile.

**The issue is not passion;
it is precision.**

A measuring cup exists for a reason. Too much sugar overwhelms the dish. Too little leaves it flat. Salt enhances flavor, but using it in excess ruins the recipe. Even the right ingredient, used carelessly, can destroy what you hoped to create.

Leadership works the same way.

Transparency, for example, is essential, but too much transparency without wisdom can create fear instead of trust. Accountability is necessary, but when over-applied without nurture, it wounds instead of strengthens. Faith fuels perseverance, but faith without follow-through becomes hollow.

This is where the **THANKFUL Method** begins to take shape.

High-level excellence requires leaders to measure each attribute carefully, understanding that no ingredient works in isolation.

Transparency must be guided by humility. Nurture must be balanced with accountability. Faithfulness must remain flexible enough to adapt. Excellence is not about adding more; it is about knowing how much is enough.

Every action a leader takes adds something to the mix. Words spoken in frustration. Silence given when clarity was needed. Pressure applied too early. Grace extended too late. These choices accumulate. Over time, they shape culture more than any vision statement ever could.

Excellence requires awareness of how small decisions, repeated daily, quietly influence outcomes, whether we intend them to or not.

A great cook knows that as you prepare a meal, you also consider quality. Cheap ingredients may fill the pot, but they never satisfy expectations. The meal may look complete, but the taste falls short. Likewise, organizations experience disappointment when leaders cut corners in their own character, standards, or development.

**Shortcuts save time,
but they cost trust.**

Excellence, whether in the kitchen or the boardroom, is not something you turn on when expectations rise. It is formed long before anyone is watching. The way we measure, prepare, and handle small moments reflects the standards we live by when the pressure is low. Long before excellence shows up in cubicles, teams, or organizations, it is introduced in everyday moments that seem small at the time but quietly shape who we become.

One of the clearest lessons I ever learned about excellence did not come from a leadership book or a workplace experience. It came from my role at home.

My life changed when my wife and I had our daughter. She is my only daughter and, without question, my favorite. From the moment she could walk, I made a quiet decision. Every door she encountered in my presence, I would open for her. From as early as two years old, I wanted her to understand her value. I wanted her to experience this not just in words, but through my consistent action. I wanted her to know that, as long as she showed up and tried, doors would open. That was the first lesson. After all, value is modeled before it is understood.

The second lesson focused on persistence. I opened doors for her, but I also watched closely as she grew. I wanted her to learn that when she strives, when she pushes herself to become who she was raised to be, doors don't just open, they open wide enough for her to walk through with confidence. Excellence creates access. It always will.

There was another standard I was setting for her. After all, I knew that one day, someone would want her time, her attention, and her heart. I wanted her to know that if someone truly valued her, they would take the time to open doors for her as well. Excellence teaches people how to treat you, and the standards we set silently demand respect.

That is when I realized something powerful. A high level of excellence does not start at work. It is introduced at home. If standards and foundations do not already exist, they cannot be created on the fly when you walk into an organization and attempt to install a culture you have never lived.

When leaders demand excellence at work without having first embodied it in their own lives, the standard collapses under pressure. Just like a meal prepared without care or attention to detail, leadership without excellence may look complete on the surface, but it will never deliver the experience it promised. Excellence must be measured, repeated, and protected ingredient-by-ingredient until it becomes the aroma that draws people in and keeps them coming back.

High-level excellence demands discipline. It requires leaders to slow down long enough to measure their responses. To pause before reacting. To ask not just what needs to be done, but how it will be received. Precision is not control. It is care. It communicates respect for those who must live with the outcome of your decisions.

Now, it is fair to note that excellence in leadership is often misunderstood. Many believe it begins with a bold vision or flawless strategy. Vision matters, but it does not sustain excellence. High-level excellence is maintained through consistent attention to people. Vision gives direction. Precision gives credibility. Without care for people, even the strongest vision eventually collapses.

Leaders must maintain altitude and awareness simultaneously. Seeing the big picture while remaining grounded in daily reality is difficult, but necessary. Distance creates blind spots. Presence reveals truth.

**Excellence is not found above the work.
It is found within it.**

You and I know that organizations rarely fail because of poor ideas. Instead, they fail because the individuals within that space feel unseen, unheard, and undervalued. A leader can articulate a compelling future and still lose commitment if the humans in the room feel ignored. People are not resources to be managed. They are individuals to be led. When leaders measure their actions with people in mind, performance rises naturally.

Excellence lives in the details that others tend to overlook. How leaders greet their teams. How they handle mistakes. How they respond when pressure increases. These moments seem small, but they shape culture in powerful ways. Consistency, not intensity, defines excellence.

Standards matter. Excellence does not mean lowering expectations to keep people comfortable. It means raising people through clarity, support, and accountability. Leaders who pursue excellence do not avoid difficult conversations. They engage them with respect. They correct without humiliating. They challenge without discouraging.

From here, we see a ripple effect. Trust grows anywhere that excellence is practiced well. Trust creates safety, which fuels creativity and ownership. When people know they are valued beyond output, they take risks, share ideas, and commit fully. Excellence thrives in environments where people feel protected while being challenged.

Attention to people requires recognizing differences. No two team members are motivated or respond to pressure in the same way. High-level leaders must measure their approach and adjust communication accordingly. They position people in roles and responsibilities where they can thrive. Excellence is not uniformity. It is alignment.

Yet when it comes to alignment, this does not mean we overlook poor performance or biting attitudes for the sake of keeping the peace. After all, culture is shaped by what leaders tolerate. Disrespect ignored becomes acceptable, which rots teams from the inside. When inconsistency is excused or normal, morale will plummet. For this reason, excellence requires leaders to summon the courage to address issues early, not to control any individual or group, but to protect the team's health. Precision applied early prevents damage later.

Consistency, even when correcting, is another indicator of excellence. Teams do not flourish under unpredictable leadership. When expectations shift based on mood or circumstance, trust erodes. Leaders who show up the same in calm, conflict, or crisis give the gift of stability. Stability then allows teams to focus on execution rather than on uncertainty.

This stability comes from a leader's actions and their intentional listening to their team's concerns and thoughts. Listening is a critical measurement tool. Leaders who listen gain insight. Those who do not rely on assumptions can hear the deeper insights that are not always articulated as clearly as they could be. Therefore, listening shows investment while also creating space for honesty, innovation,and accountability. When people feel heard, commitment deepens.

Excellence grows when dialogue replaces directives.

Many of us have been in situations where recognition is overlooked. Yet this key element is essential. Our team members do not need constant praise, but they do need acknowledgment. Recognition affirms effort and reinforces values. Leaders who measure progress, not just perfection, sustain momentum. Encouragement fuels perseverance, while letting people know they are on the right track.

Excellence also requires knowing when to step back. Micromanagement suffocates growth. Precision is not equal to control. It is better defined as trust applied wisely. Empowered teams develop ownership. Leaders who release control strategically multiply their impact.

With all these factors at hand, we might wonder what sustains excellence. For me, it is reflection. By looking at ourselves and taking time to pause, we get to self-assess if we are showing up in the way we intend to. Without pausing, it is easy to drift slowly. Self-examination keeps us aligned. Questions like: "How am I showing up?" "What am I tolerating?" and "Where do I need to grow?" prevent an erosion of standards. Excellence is maintained through humility and honesty.

The **THANKFUL Method** becomes tangible in this chapter. This is our first chance to create our own blend of each attribute, carefully applying each one as needed. We get to have transparency measured with humility, faithfulness balanced with adaptability, and nurturing guided by accountability.

Excellence emerges as we use each ingredient with restraint and wisdom, as the circumstance calls for a unique blend each time.

Leadership excellence is not perfection. It is intentionality. It means choosing accuracy over impulse, discipline over convenience, and care over speed. Leaders who practice high-level excellence understand that relationships and results are inseparable.

Ultimately, our own aim for excellence will be measured by impact. This is not just about numbers. Instead, it is about lives influenced, confidence built, and potential unlocked. When we measure and utilize each ingredient in the **THANKFUL Method** well, our teams endure, organizations last, and legacies form.

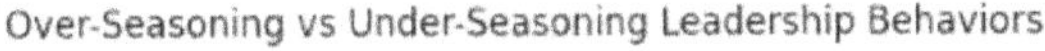

Over-Seasoning vs Under-Seasoning Leadership Behaviors

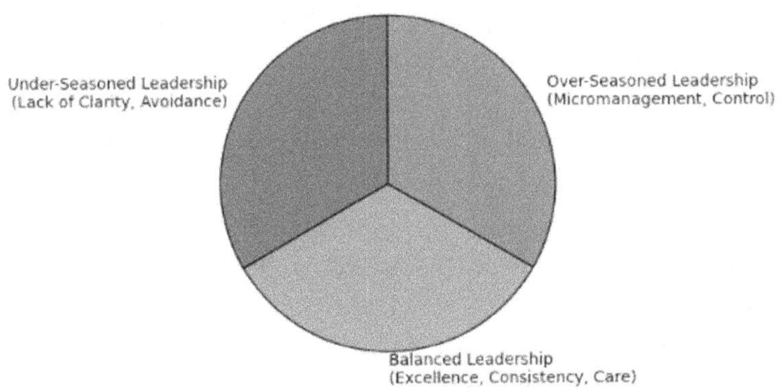

Excellence in leadership is not loud. It does not rush the stove or turn the heat all the way up just to prove something is happening. Excellence knows when to simmer. It understands that flavor develops over time, not through force.

Anyone can turn up the heat. Yet few have the discipline to wait.

Great leaders learn when to add and when to step back. Too much seasoning overwhelms the dish. Too little makes it forgettable. Excellence lives in the space between urgency and patience. It pays attention and tastes along the way. It adjusts before damage is done. That is the difference between cooking to impress and cooking to serve.

The leaders who get this right do not chase applause. They focus on consistency. They show up every day to the same kitchen, with the same care, even when no one is watching. They understand that excellence is not defined by a single moment. It is built quietly, decision-by-decision, long before the meal is served.

When excellence leads, people feel it before they can explain it. The culture feels steady. The expectations are clear. The team trusts the process because they trust the person guiding it. Like a well-prepared meal, nothing feels rushed, forced, or forgotten. Everything belongs.

Excellence is never about perfection. It is about intention, honoring the process, and refusing to cut corners even when you are tired. It means understanding that if we rush now, the entire dish will suffer later.

In the end, leadership excellence is measured the same way a great meal is remembered. The delight never comes from how quickly the dish was made, but by how it made people feel. We feel most cared for when we are nourished and valued. That is when we are ready to come back for more.

That is the standard of excellence I am calling us to aim for. Why? *Because it is an aroma worth creating.*

The THANKFUL Blend:
This Week in the Kitchen

Excellence is not built in theory. It is formed in small, repeatable actions taken when no one is applauding. This is where leadership shifts from intention to practice. If you want a different culture, you must first change how you show up in ordinary moments.

This week, I want you to step into the kitchen intentionally. Not to overhaul everything, but to measure one ingredient at a time. Think of this exercise as practice, not performance.

T , Transparency (Measured, Not Dumped)

Action Step:
This week, choose one moment where you would normally withhold clarity to avoid discomfort. Instead, offer honest, calm communication with care.

- Say what needs to be said without oversharing.
- Be clear without being harsh.
- Ask yourself: Is this helpful, or am I just venting?

Transparency builds trust when it is paired with wisdom.

H , Humility (Lower the Heat)

Action Step:
Identify one interaction where you will intentionally listen more than you speak.

- Ask a question and resist the urge to correct.
- Acknowledge someone else's perspective, even if you disagree.
- If appropriate, admit where you don't have all the answers.

> Humility does not weaken leadership.
> It stabilizes it.

A , Accountability (Season with Care)

Action Step:
Address one small issue early instead of letting it grow.
- Be direct, but respectful.
- Focus on behavior, not character.
- Clearly state expectations moving forward.

> Accountability applied early prevents damage later.
> Silence is not kindness.

N , Nurture (Reinforce the Right Behavior)

Action Step:
Offer one specific encouragement this week.

- Affirm a behavior, not just the result.
- Connect someone's effort to values.
- Keep your comments genuine and timely.

People repeat what is recognized.
Nurture reinforces culture.

K , Knowledge (Taste as You Go)

Action Step:
Pause at the end of the week and reflect.
Ask yourself:

- What worked this week?
- What felt off?
- What will I adjust next time?

Growth requires reflection.
Leaders who never taste the dish cannot improve it.

F , Faithfulness (Stay in the Kitchen)

This is where most leaders drift. Not because they lack vision , but because they lack endurance.

Action Step:
Choose consistency over convenience.

- Show up with the same care, even when tired.
- Follow through on one promise you've been tempted to delay.
- Revisit one commitment you quietly allowed to slip.
- Ask: If my team experienced this version of me every day, would trust grow or shrink?

Deeper Reflection Questions:

- Where am I strong when visible but inconsistent when unseen?
- Have I allowed fatigue to become an excuse for unreliability?
- What would it look like to finish this season well?

Faithfulness is rarely celebrated loudly
, but it is always felt deeply.
It is the ingredient that turns potential
into credibility.

U , Understanding (Adjust the Blend)

Leadership is not just about what you say. It is about how it lands.

Action Step:
Pay attention to one person's response to your leadership this week.

- Are they leaning in or withdrawing?
- Are they energized or guarded?
- Did your tone match your intention?
- Ask them directly: How can I support you better right now?

Deeper Reflection Questions:

- What assumptions am I making about this person?
- Am I leading them the way I prefer to be led , or the way they need?
- Have I confused agreement with understanding?

> Understanding requires emotional attentiveness.
> You cannot adjust what you refuse to notice.

L , Leadership (Serve the Table, Not the Ego)

Action Step:
Make one decision this week that benefits the team more than it benefits you.

- Share credit.
- Take responsibility.
- Protect the culture even when it costs you comfort.

> Leadership is proven in what
> you are willing to sacrifice.

A Final Challenge:

Do not attempt to perfect every ingredient this week. That is not excellence, that is overwhelming. Choose one or two actions and commit fully. Repeat them. Measure them. Reflect on them.

Excellence is built the same way great meals are made, not in a rush, not by accident, and never all at once. Stay in the kitchen. The aroma is forming.

Chapter 3 Reflection:

- Where do I tend to over-season my leadership?
- Where have I under-seasoned accountability or care?
- How do my daily behaviors shape culture?
- Within my leadership choices, what attributes do I need to measure with great care?

When The Cook Forgets To Eat

A kitchen can be full, busy, and productive meals going out, plates being filled, people being served, yet the one preparing it all quietly goes without. The cook tastes along the way, adjusts the seasoning, ensures everything is right for everyone else, but never sits long enough to receive what they've created. Over time, the kitchen begins to run on depletion instead of intention. And what once came from care slowly starts coming from exhaustion. Because when the kitchen serves everyone but the cook, it is only a matter of time before what is being prepared loses its strength.

And leadership works the same way.

If you are not willing to work through pain, then let me tell you a hard truth. Leadership may not be for you. There will be seasons when your family is upset with you, your spouse is disappointed, your supervisor is silent, and your team wants nothing to do with you, all at the same time. Leadership does not conveniently space out hardship. It stacks it.

When you accepted the call to lead, you probably imagined good days, smiling faces, and a team that was already aligned and motivated. You thought leadership meant progress without resistance. That belief usually comes from forgetting to read the fine print. The fine print reads something like this: *Dear future leader, thank you for accepting this call. Please understand that everyone who came before you has been disappointed, misunderstood, wounded, and at times lost themselves for the good of others. If you are still willing to accept this role, sign your name and move forward.*

I write this half-jokingly. But in all honesty, the sentiment deserves to be stated to anyone thinking of taking a position of leadership.

In my time, I have watched leaders cry behind closed doors. I have seen marriages strained, children grow distant, milestones missed, and mistakes repeated publicly. Leadership costs something. Average leaders feel the pain and keep moving without reflection. Good leaders pause, learn, and refuse to make the same mistake twice. They climb out of the hole they helped to dig and then build a bridge for others to cross.

Leadership and sacrifice are inseparable. It is like seeing a house on fire and grabbing a hose to save it, knowing you will have to run barefoot over hot coals to reach the flames. The outcome matters. The people matter. The house may be saved. But the pain in putting out the fire is real, and the cost is personal.

Leadership is not about avoiding the fire. It is about deciding if the rescue is worth the burn.

But here is where many leaders lose themselves: they begin to believe they must run into every fire.

Courage can slowly become compulsion. Responsibility can quietly become identity. What begins as a noble sacrifice can turn into constant self-neglect. And over time, a leader who once chose the burn intentionally begins living in it permanently.

Sacrifice is part of leadership. But there are limits.

A knife was never meant to replace a spoon. Each has a distinct purpose, and each plays a necessary role in preparing a meal. A knife cuts and divides. A spoon gathers and nourishes. When one is forced to do the other's work, the meal suffers. This fact does not indicate that either tool lacks value. Instead, the struggle is proof that they are being used outside their design. Leadership works the same way. When one role begins to replace every other calling in our lives, something essential is lost.

Salt and pepper were created to complement each other, not compete. Salt brings out what is already present. Pepper adds depth and contrast. Used together, they elevate the dish. Used excessively, they overwhelm it. Many leaders believe that the more time, availability, and access they give of themselves to others means those people will always produce better results. But excess, even when rooted in service, eventually undermines what it was meant to enhance.

Water and ice come from the same source, yet they serve different purposes. Water restores. Ice preserves. But each has its time and place. Water that remains frozen cannot quench our thirst. Leaders hardened by responsibility, pressure, and expectation may continue to function, but they slowly lose the ability to feel, connect, and heal. Faith reminds us that leadership was never meant to be sustained by strength alone, but by renewal.

Leadership, like a well-prepared meal, depends on the right ingredients used in the right measure. Purpose provides direction. Faith provides grounding. Presence gives meaning to both. When one responsibility becomes everything, the rest of life begins to shrink. Therefore, we must examine the quiet cost of misplaced devotion and return to a healthier, more faithful way of leading, one that honors both the work entrusted to us and the people we are called to love.

Growing up, my father worked tirelessly to ensure our family always had food on the table. His commitment was unquestionable. His work ethic was unmatched. But that provision came at a cost. From as early as I can remember, he was rarely able to attend school programs, sporting events, or milestones my sisters and I reached. While other children scanned the crowd looking for familiar faces, I simply did not look at all. Over time, the hope of seeing him in the stands faded quietly, and I learned to manage my disappointment internally.

As a child, I could not understand how a father could miss so many moments and still love his children. In my young mind, presence equaled care, and absence felt like indifference. I promised myself that when I had a family of my own, I would never miss a game, performance, or milestone. I told myself that work would never take priority over my children, the way it seemed to have for him.

But in my young heart and mind, I missed something. I did not see how hard my father was working on my behalf, seeking to provide a life and countless opportunities for me. What I did not yet understand from my father's example was the power of sacrifice.

As I grew older, that perspective replaced the assumptions I had about my father. I began to understand that sacrifice is unavoidable in leadership.

But on the other hand, we must remember that misplaced sacrifice is destructive. Leaders give. Leaders pour out. Leaders are stretched. But family should never become collateral damage in the pursuit of titles, influence, or approval.

My father did not chase applause. He did not hunger for titles, status, or the spotlight. What he pursued was responsibility. And responsibility required sacrifice. It meant long hours. It meant absence. It meant providing even when it cost him presence.

As a child, I did not always understand it. I only felt the distance. But as a man, I see the weight he carried. He was not climbing ladders for recognition; he was carrying a family on his shoulders.

But for those of us who are away not because we must provide, but because we are chasing the next rung, the next title, the next promotion , perhaps it is time to pause. Because there is a difference between sacrifice and ambition.

Responsibility builds.
Ego consumes.

And the ladder we are climbing may one day lean against the wrong wall , while the people who matter most are standing at the bottom, waiting for us to come home. After all, we often spend more waking hours with our teams than with our families.

Therefore, we must ask ourselves a painfully simple question: *What is the point of sacrificing your family for a role if distance and absence cost you the very people you claim to be doing it for?*

During my career, I have served on multiple boards. At one point, I was Chair of four boards and Co-Chair of five more. My calendar was full. My phone never stopped ringing. I was always needed somewhere. I ran from meeting to meeting, which meant I arrived late to my children's basketball and baseball games. I ate dinner at nine o'clock more times than I could count. Somewhere along the way, a sobering realization settled in. My salary was changing, but so were my children. Promotions could wait. Childhood could not.

I did not want my children to grow up scanning the stands the way I once did. I did not want them learning how to manage disappointment in silence. Leadership success means nothing if it costs you connection where it matters most.

My entire adult life, my mother called often, and no matter how the conversation began, it always ended the same way. "Son, I don't have any money, but what I do have is prayer." Those words carried weight I would not fully understand until later.

Then, in 2022, my mother's health declined.

Three years later, I was on my way to my first evaluation at a new job. I was proud of the progress our team had made and was optimistic about the future. On the way to the meeting, my father called. He told me my mother was not doing well and was back in the hospital. It was a call I had received many times over the past few years. I told him I would call back after my evaluation.

The meeting went well. We shared laughs, discussed vision, and celebrated progress. As I stepped into the golf cart afterward, my phone rang again. It was my father. His voice was different this time. "Son," he said, "your mom just passed."

In an instant, everything stopped.

One moment, I was celebrating progress. Next, my world shifted completely. Tears came without warning. My chest felt hollow. Time slowed yet somehow rushed forward all at once.

I called each of my sisters because my father could not bring himself to do it.

Four phone calls.
Four moments of heartbreak.
Four times I had to find words that did not exist.

With each call, the weight grew heavier. I could hear it in their silence before the tears came. I could feel my own voice shaking as I tried to be steady for them when I was anything but steady myself. By the time the last call ended, I was empty.

I returned to my office and sat down, staring at nothing. I couldn't cry freely. I couldn't think clearly. I just sat there, broken, trying to breathe through a moment that did not feel real.

One of my team members walked in and said nothing. They simply sat with me. No advice. No agenda. Just presence. Eventually, my wife arrived to take me home. I remember her walking in, seeing my face, and knowing immediately that I was not okay. I couldn't drive. I didn't trust myself to be behind the wheel.

As we pulled onto the road, the tears came in waves. I covered my face with my hands, wiping them away, trying to steady myself. And then, as if the day hadn't already taken enough, the car began to overheat. We had to pull over.

In that moment, everything felt like it was going wrong at once.

I remember sitting there on the side of the road, overwhelmed and confused, asking myself how a day that started so normal had turned so heavy so quickly. Grief does that. It disorients you. It doesn't knock, it just enters.

When we finally made it home, I sat quietly. I had no time to collapse completely, because that evening my oldest son had his high school baccalaureate service, a church service honoring graduating seniors just days before commencement.

Every part of me wanted to stay home, to sink into the couch, and to let grief have its way. But I refused to let absence write another chapter in my family's story.

When I was his age, my father missed events like this. Not because he didn't care, but because life, work, and responsibility always seemed to pull him elsewhere. I had promised myself that my story would be different.

So I gathered myself. Not because I was strong, but because my son needed me present.

We walked into the church, and people greeted me warmly. Then it began.

One person needed a favor.
Another wanted to schedule a meeting.
Someone handed me a phone to review transcripts.

And I did it all. I smiled. I responded. I showed up for everyone.

Then I sat down. And something inside me broke open.

For years, I had been everything to everyone. And on the worst day of my adult life, I had become nothing to myself.

I realized in that moment how dangerous unchecked availability can be. How leadership can quietly train you to believe that being needed is the same as being valued. How easily responsibility can crowd out humanity.

Leadership rarely pauses to ask if we are okay. We are expected to show up, push forward, and carry others even when our own strength is gone. We celebrate excellence while ignoring exhaustion. We applaud resilience while overlooking the cost.

Here is the truth I learned that day. Excellence is a mirage if it costs you your soul. Leadership is not about endless availability. It is about responsible presence.

If you lose yourself, you eventually lose your ability to lead anyone else well.

Unchecked availability is not faithfulness. It is an imbalance. When everyone has access to you, no one truly has you. Boundaries are not barriers. They are safeguards. They protect your family, your faith, your health, and your calling.

Leadership will quietly convince you that being needed is the same as being valued. It is not. Being needed feeds ego. Being present builds legacy. Titles open doors, but presence opens hearts.

True leadership knows when to stand strong for others and when to sit still for yourself. It understands that you cannot pour endlessly without being refilled. When one becomes everything to everyone, one risks becoming nothing to themselves.

And no position, platform, or promotion is worth that cost.

If I could go back to that moment, I would have done a few things differently.

I would have taken five more minutes with my father.

I would have asked him to let me hear my mother's voice one more time, through his memories.

I would have thanked her out loud for every lesson she ever taught me, even the ones I didn't understand at the time.

I would have slowed my conversations with team members and leaders, remembering that the person standing in front of me chose to bring something to me, time, trust, vulnerability, or perspective. And that sometimes, that conversation might be the last one we ever have.

I thought I already valued patience. That day taught me to value presence.

An Invitation to You

And you, dear reader, deserve to hear this:

It is okay to pause.
It is okay to say, "Not right now."
It is okay to protect moments that matter.

This week, I invite you to do one small thing differently.

Take five extra minutes with someone you love.

Be fully present in one conversation that you would normally rush.

Set one boundary that protects your soul instead of your schedule.

Leadership is not proven by how much you can carry. It is revealed by what you choose not to drop.

Be present while you still can. That is excellence worth protecting.

Chapter 4 Reflection

- Where has availability replaced presence in my life?
- What relationships are paying the cost of my leadership?
- How does my faith inform my boundaries?
- What would a responsible presence look like this season?

You Will Get Cut

Have you ever prepared a meal you knew by heart? One you could make without thinking about measurements or timers because you have done it so many times before. You know where every ingredient goes. You know the ratio. You know the timing. Yet no matter how familiar a recipe is, if you use a knife and take your eyes off the task, even for a moment, you will get cut.

Familiarity does not remove danger.
Comfort does not eliminate consequence.

Leadership works the same way. Experience does not make us immune to pain. Titles do not protect us from wounds. In fact, the longer we lead, the sharper others' tools become. Expectations grow. Influence increases. Responsibility deepens. And while leadership comes with its share of bumps, bruises, scratches, and cuts, the wounds that cut deepest are the ones we help create.

Some cuts come from careless decisions. Others come from misplaced trust. Occasionally, a well-intentioned development conversation can damage us if someone approaches without discernment, preparation, or prayer.

It is time to name this reality plainly: If you lead long enough, you will get cut. The question is whether those cuts will sharpen you or scar you.

Early in my leadership journey, I participated in several leadership development programs. We read books, completed assessments, and spent hours discussing growth and influence. Eventually, the moment came. We had all anticipated it. The facilitator told us: "Now it is time to find a mentor. Choose someone you admire. Look for someone who is already doing what you aspire to do, someone whose seat you hope to sit in one day."

Everyone already had their top choice. There was always one leader everyone wanted to learn from. But when we realized that the leader could only take one or two people, panic set in. Suddenly, second and third choices felt like consolation prizes. Still, you made a selection and endured an awkward first meeting. Realizing it was an opportunity more than an assignment, you met regularly. Months turned into years. And if you were fortunate, that relationship became lifelong. I am grateful to the individuals who invested time in me. What started as an unfamiliar process became something that helped to anchor me in my own leadership. What no one prepared me for, however, was the moment the roles would reverse.

Eventually, the mentee becomes the one being sought out as a mentor. People begin asking you for guidance, time, access, and wisdom. In that process, I realized that conversations were growing heavier. Situations became personal. Crises appeared without warning. And one critical truth became painfully clear.

If you do not become intentional and discerning about who you mentor, you will get cut.

I learned this lesson the hard way.

There was a young leader I poured into for years. I saw potential in him before he saw it in himself. I gave him access to my time, my counsel, my network. I brought him into rooms he had not earned yet because I believed exposure would accelerate his growth. I defended him in meetings when others questioned his readiness. I corrected him privately. I championed him publicly.

And for a while, he grew. But growth without character reinforcement is unstable. Ambition without maturity is sharp.

Over time, I began noticing subtle shifts. Conversations became transactional. Gratitude turned into entitlement. Advice was no longer received; it was tolerated. I dismissed the warning signs because I was emotionally invested. I had poured too much in to believe it could turn.

Then one day, it did.

A decision was made behind my back. A narrative was shaped that excluded context. Private conversations were leveraged for personal advancement. In a single moment, I realized I had not just mentored a leader, I had empowered someone who had not yet learned loyalty.

It felt like a clean slice. Not loud. Not dramatic. Just sharp.

The pain was not professional. It was personal. I wasn't wounded because strategy failed. I was wounded because trust gave out.

That is the cut no one prepares you for.

Mentorship requires vulnerability. You open doors. You share failures. You expose lessons learned in private battles. And when that openness is mishandled, it stings in a way metrics never could.

But here is the deeper truth. The pain did not mean mentorship was wrong. It meant discernment was missing.

A chef handles knives daily. The knife is not evil. It is necessary. It prepares the meal. But if you handle it carelessly or hand it to someone untrained, there will be blood.

Mentorship is the same.

You cannot stop mentoring because you were cut. But you must learn to discern readiness before you give access. Not everyone who asks for proximity is prepared for responsibility. Not everyone who admires your platform can steward your principles.

The purpose of mentorship is multiplication. The pain of poor discernment is betrayal.

And if you lead long enough, you will experience both.

Being a mentor carries weight. I have come to see it as a sacred responsibility. As individuals approached me, I became sober to the fact that someone was entrusting me with their growth, their questions, and often their future. They see something in us they want to learn from, something they hope to emulate. Therefore, I cannot view mentorship as something that is casual. Instead, it is covenantal, something that requires time, consistency, and honesty.

This is where the **THANKFUL Method** matters deeply. Each ingredient matters. A mentor must be transparent, not curated. Humble, not defensive. Adaptable, not rigid. A nurturer, not a controller. A kneeler, not a self-made expert. Faithful, not convenient. A unifier, not a divider. Loyal, not self-serving.

Mentorship without these ingredients is not incomplete; it is dangerous.

The transition from mentee to mentor does not happen with a title or a single meeting request. It happens quietly, over time, through faithfulness in small things. A mentee becomes a mentor when they stop chasing proximity to influence and start stewarding the lessons they have been given. Knowledge alone does not qualify someone to lead. Wisdom does. And wisdom is formed through obedience, humility, and lived experience.

The best mentees are not those who simply absorb information, but those who apply it with integrity. They listen closely, ask honest questions, and practice what they are taught even when no one is watching. Over time, their character begins to speak louder than their ambition. Trust follows. Influence appears before authority ever does.

This transition requires a shift in posture. A mentee often looks upward, focused on learning and receiving. A mentor must look outward, focused on serving and giving. That shift only happens when the ego is surrendered. The mentee who becomes a mentor understands the fact that leadership is not about being impressive; it is about being responsible. They stop asking: What will this role give me? Instead, they ask: *Who am I called to help?*

Faith plays a critical role in this process. A kneeling leader understands they do not mentor from their own strength, but from what God has shaped in them through pressure, correction, and grace. The mentee who is becoming a mentor learns to pray not only for their own personal growth, but also for the growth of others. They begin carrying people in prayer long before carrying them in responsibility.

Eventually, a mentee becomes a mentor when they realize they will one day be accountable not only for what they learned, but for what they passed on. Mentorship is stewardship. What you receive is never meant to stop with you. When embraced with transparency, humility, adaptability, and faithfulness, mentorship multiplies impact far beyond personal reach.

You cannot plant bad seeds and expect a good harvest. Whatever you pour into someone will grow. The question is what they will become.

I call this the Mentee Tree.

Every mentor grows one. You do not measure a mentor by their platform. You measure them by their fruit.

The Mentee Tree is living evidence of your leadership. It is not found in your résumé, your title, or your applause. It is found in the people who once sat across from you, asking questions, and are now standing on their own, making decisions.

Some trees bear fruit. Others grow thorns. But every tree reveals its roots.

A sign of a good mentor is not how many people claim them. It is how many people flourish because of them. When you look back years later, can you point to leaders who are whole, ethical, and steady? Can you see families strengthened, organizations improved, and character preserved?

Or do you see ambition without integrity? Influence without loyalty? Talent without humility?

Time determines the harvest.

The fruit your mentees produce will eventually speak on your behalf. Not perfectly. Not completely. But powerfully.

And this is why mentorship must never be casual.

**You are not just offering advice.
You are planting seeds.**

If those within your realm of influence are struggling and you have not noticed, that matters. If they failed and you have not followed up, that matters. If you never seem to have time for them, that matters. If you gave advice without prayer, direction without care, or access without accountability, that matters. If you are not prepared to take responsibility for your influence, stepping back from mentorship may be the most loving decision you can make.

Not everyone is called to mentor in every season. This is not failure. It is wisdom. It is far better to say no or not right now than to say yes and harm someone through neglect, inconsistency, or ego. Poor mentorship cuts deeper than no mentorship at all.

For those of us who choose to mentor, we understand this clearly. We will get hurt. We will be misunderstood. We may be lied about. We may pour into someone who walks away ungrateful or unchanged. That is part of the cost. But when done with discernment, prayer, and purpose, I have found mentorship to be one of the most powerful expressions of leadership.

Faith reminds us that we always carry the role of student and teacher at the same time. We need mentors who sharpen us, and we must become mentors who steward our influence wisely. When mentorship is grounded in the **THANKFUL Method**, keeping each ingredient as part of a daily recipe, it produces leaders who are not only capable but whole.

So choose carefully whom you are influenced by and who you influence. Pray often. Lead humbly. And keep your eyes on the blade. Because in leadership, you will get cut. The goal is not to avoid it, but to ensure it shapes you rather than destroys you.

Reflection Questions:
Examining Mentorship Wounds

It is our duty to ensure that we do not lead out of pain or woundedness. Hurt people hurt people, and we must avoid passing on brokenness. The good news? We can seek restoration and become whole. When we do, we get to pass on not only lessons but a path to pursue wholeness.

To begin, let's reflect on our own stories, and ensure that we can process any pain we are carrying.

These questions are designed to surface wounds honestly, not to assign blame, but to invite healing, wisdom, and growth.

1.   Who has mentored me in the past and left a scar? What growth did those relationships leave behind?

2.   Have I ever been hurt by a mentor's absence, inconsistency, ego, or lack of care? How did that experience shape the way I now lead?

3.   In what ways might I have unintentionally wounded someone I mentored?

4.   Are there mentorship relationships I entered too quickly, without prayer or discernment?

5.   When conflict or disappointment arose with a mentee, did I respond with humility or defensiveness?

6.   Have I ever continued mentoring out of obligation rather than out of a calling?

7.   What cuts from leadership have sharpened me, and
        which ones still need healing?

8.   Do I create space for honest feedback from those
        I mentor, or do I assume silence means satisfaction?

9.   Have I ever avoided a hard conversation with a
        mentee to protect my image?

10.   What patterns do I see when I reflect on my
        "mentee tree"? Growth, stagnation, or distance?

I invite you to take time with these questions. I have learned
firsthand that leadership wounds ignored tend to reopen. Yet
leadership wounds, once examined, mature into wisdom.

Who Gets Access?
Choosing Who Gets Access to Your Kitchen

Not everyone who asks for mentorship is ready for access.

Just as not every ingredient belongs in every meal, not every aspiring leader is prepared for proximity. Mentorship is not casual. It is covenantal. When you allow someone into your leadership space, you are not just sharing advice. You are sharing patterns. You are sharing convictions. You are sharing the private disciplines that built your public influence.

And if you open your kitchen too quickly, you will get cut.

There is a difference between someone who is hungry to grow and someone who is hungry to be seen. The two can look similar at first. Both ask questions. Both show enthusiasm. Both talk about vision. But over time, character reveals motive.

Mentorship is not about managing potential. It is about multiplying character.

Before you say yes to mentoring someone, pause long enough to ask the deeper questions. Not the flattering ones. The formative ones.

Because access is powerful. And power handed to someone prematurely becomes a weapon.

Step One: Confirm the Season

Every leader goes through seasons.
There are seasons for learning.

Seasons for pruning.
Seasons for rebuilding.
And seasons for leading others.

Do not confuse ambition with readiness.

Ask yourself:

- Is this person in a season of humility or urgency?
- Are they seeking development or acceleration?
- Are they willing to grow slowly, or do they only want quick exposure?

Even the best ingredients spoil if placed under pressure too soon. If someone is still wrestling with insecurity, ego, inconsistency, or unhealed wounds, mentorship will not fix that. Instead, it may expose it.

Mentorship requires margin. It requires teachability and stability.

If a potential mentee is not faithful where they currently are, it is ill-advised to promote them into proximity.

Step Two: Evaluate Alignment with the THANKFUL Method

You cannot multiply what you do not see.

Before someone sits at your table, observe their life, and not just their performance.

Are they:

- Transparent or not polished?
- Humble or defensive?
- Adaptable, or reactive?
- Nurturing or transactional?
- A kneeler or self-reliant?
- Faithful or convenient?
- A unifier or easily divided?
- Loyal or strategic with relationships?

You are not looking for perfection. You are looking for consistency.

If these ingredients are not already present in seed form, mentorship will not plant them. It will only amplify what is already growing.

Do not hand someone your recipe if they have not first demonstrated the fact they respect the kitchen.

Step Three: Look for Evidence, Not Potential

Potential is important when hiring. Evidence is critical in mentorship. A mentor should already be living what they are teaching. Evaluating how they treat people who cannot help them gives us insight into their character. By observing how they respond under pressure, we see what attributes they would pass on. Pay attention to how they speak about past teams and leaders to gain insight on how they are likely to speak about you and your circle.

Potential is attractive. Evidence is safer.

**We hire for potential.
We mentor for evidence.**

Watch how they treat people who cannot help them.
Watch how they respond to correction.
Watch how they speak about former leaders.

Consider: *Do they leave relationships intact, or do they leave confusion behind them?*

Fruit tells the truth.

A good mentee leaves a trail of growth.
A dangerous one leaves a trail of blame.

If you see weeds, do not call it fruit just because you want it to grow.

Step Four: Assess How They Handle the Knife

Mentorship sharpens people.

It gives them language.
It gives them confidence.
It gives them access.
It gives them influence.

You are not just giving advice. You are placing sharper tools in their hands.

Ask yourself:

- When this person gains power, will they protect people , or position them for success?
- When they are corrected, do they soften, or harden?
- When they are entrusted with confidential insight, do they guard it, or leverage it?

A knife in steady hands prepares a meal.
A knife in careless hands wounds those in the kitchen.

If you see recklessness now, it will not disappear later.

Step Five: Confirm Their Willingness, Not Just Their Skill

Some people want proximity.
Few want process.

Have the courageous conversation.

Ask them:

- Are you willing to be corrected?
- Are you willing to be unseen while you grow?
- Are you willing to wait for your turn?
- Are you willing to be faithful in obscurity?

Their answers will tell you everything.

Mentorship must be chosen, not assumed. If someone hesitates when commitment is required, honor that hesitation. It is better to tell someone that this is "not their season" than to say "yes" and leave room for them to cause damage.

Forced mentorship produces fragile leaders.
Patient, vetted mentorship produces good fruit.

Mentorship Is Stewardship

Being a mentor is not flattering. It is weighty.

When someone approaches you for guidance, they are entrusting you with influence over their decisions, their mindset, and sometimes even advice about their family. That is sacred.

This is why discernment matters.

You will still get hurt at some point in the process.

Even with prayer.
Even with wisdom.
Even with preparation.

But there is a difference between wounds that refine you and wounds that could have been prevented.

**Discernment does not eliminate pain.
It reduces unnecessary bleeding.**

Examine Your Mentee Tree

Every mentor has a mentee tree.

Definition: *A mentee tree is the living evidence of your influence. Its branches are formed by the leaders who have grown from your investment and the fruit their lives now produce.*

Some trees are healthy.
Some are diseased.
Some are neglected.
Some are flourishing.

But every mentor has one.

Here is the saying I live by:

"The true measure of a mentor is not their platform, but the fruit their mentee tree produces."

Step back and examine yours. Where are the people you have poured into?

Are they growing in character?
Are they unified?
Are they faithful?

Are they multiplying what was given to them, or distorting it? Time will always reveal what your investment produced.

If you see unhealthy fruit, do not rush to blame the branch. Reflect on your influence. Ask what seed was planted. Ask what you tolerated. Ask what you ignored. Ask where discernment was absent.

This is not condemnation.
It is calibration.

This is crucial because mentorship is multiplication.

And multiplication magnifies everything, good or bad.

Why This Matters

Many leaders talk about mentorship. Few approach it with this level of intentionality. Organizations want development pipelines. Leaders want succession plans.

But what we truly need are discerning relationships grounded in character, prayer, and accountability. If you get this right, you will not just build leaders. You will build legacy. If you get this wrong, you will build a ripple effect that eventually turns on you.

My advice?

Choose carefully.
Pray consistently.
Observe patiently.

And never confuse access with readiness.

Because in leadership, you will get cut.

The goal is not to stop mentoring.
The goal is to steward it wisely.

And that begins with who you allow into your kitchen.

It's Time To Go Shopping

Before any great meal is prepared, someone must take inventory of what is in stock. You open the pantry and check the refrigerator. You assess what you already have before deciding what you need to get from the store. Some ingredients are fresh and ready to be used. Others have been sitting on the shelf for too long. They may have served their purpose in a previous season, but now they are no longer usable. Ignoring the fact that some ingredients have lost their flavor over time and using them anyway does not improve the meal. It only guarantees disappointment.

Leadership requires this same level of honesty.

Teams change. Seasons shift. What once worked well may no longer fit the direction ahead. Wise leaders are not afraid to acknowledge when an ingredient has expired. They understand that clinging to the past out of comfort, fear, or loyalty can compromise everything they are trying to build in the present.

Imagine things have been going well, and it is finally time to prepare a meal using the best ingredients in your pantry. You gather each item carefully, knowing that once everything is ready, you can roll up your sleeves and start cooking. But as you begin, you notice that one of the main ingredients has expired. Without it, the meal will not taste the same. You cannot ignore it or work around it. It would be foolish to pretend the dish will improve once heat is applied. A different course of action is needed.

Therefore, it is time to go shopping.

Leadership is paired with both celebration and loss. Sometimes one of your strongest employees is promoted within the organization or called to a new opportunity. Other times, a team member who has walked with you for a long season must be released. Leaders must remember that seasons expire, just as products on a grocery shelf do. Every effective leader learns to recognize when something essential is missing, when a position has outgrown a person, or when a person has outgrown the role.

When a team member is promoted, it should be celebrated. That is success, not loss. When a team member resigns or is released under difficult circumstances, it is still a moment to pause and reflect. These moments are never easy, but they create space to determine what the team needs next. Separating the personal from the process is critical. Letting go does not always mean you failed them. Often, it simply means the season changed.

Imagine, with me, for a moment, that you could intentionally go food shopping. You are not rushed. You are not pressured to settle. You can visit different stores, ask questions, and read labels carefully. You can be thoughtful about what you bring back into the kitchen.

Hiring works the same way. This is your opportunity to shape your team's future by choosing the right ingredient, not just the one that's available.

Some leaders spend years without an opportunity to hire anyone new. They inherit teams and never get to shop for them. I have enjoyed every team I have been part of, but I have learned one simple truth: If I lead a team and no one is promoted, recognized, or prepared to grow beyond my supervision, then I have failed them as a leader.

Leadership is not about keeping people. It is about preparing them.

Interviewing candidates, whether virtually or in person, gives leaders the opportunity to make informed choices. It is always easy to hire someone. It is far harder to let them go. That is why discernment matters so much right from the start. Rushed decisions often lead to costly corrections later.

Have you ever gone grocery shopping and realized that if you want to eat healthy, it usually costs more? The ingredients that produce better outcomes often come at a higher price. Why? Because they require more time, care, and nurturing. A farmer does not rush a crop and expect excellence. That same truth applies to leadership.

All steaks do not taste the same. All fruits do not look the same. And even seeds planted in the same soil do not grow into identical flowers. When we shop, we take time to find the right item on our list. We inspect, compare, and ask ourselves if it is worth the cost. Leadership requires the same level of care when searching for the right person to bring onto a team.

Too often, we rush the hiring process. Sadly, this is like running into the dairy section and grabbing the first gallon of milk you see, only to find out it expires in two days. If you had taken thirty more seconds, you might have noticed that the milk in the third row had an expiration date two weeks later.

Small pauses save frustration later.

Taking time during the search process protects the team, the mission, and your own credibility.

By taking your time, you have space to find what you are looking for. If the first store does not have what you need, it is okay to get back in your car and drive to the next one. That does not mean you failed; it means you are committed to getting it right. In leadership, this translates to not falling in love with the first interviewee, just because someone is willing to sit in an empty seat. It is okay to slow down, interview again, and ensure the person you bring in has culture fit. It is worth taking time to find the right ingredient for the recipe you are preparing.

I remember going grocery shopping with my dad one time. He said, "Son, go grab some eggs." I ran to the cooler, grabbed the first carton I saw, and proudly brought it back to him, happy to accomplish the task. He gazed at me and gave me the look only a father can, as he opened the carton and showed me a cracked egg inside. He told me, "If you don't open the carton and inspect the eggs before you invest, we'll get home and realize we only receive eleven eggs even though we paid for twelve, and we can never get our time back."

The image of that one cracked egg has stayed with me. From that day on, I learned to inspect what I chose. I carried that same mindset into my leadership and reflect on it when interviewing. I ask tougher questions. I check references carefully. One question I often ask candidates is, "What is a common misconception your colleagues have about you?" That question usually shocks them for a moment. It forces honesty. It reveals self-awareness. For me, this is less about trapping them by revealing something unpleasant. Instead, it helps me to determine whether this person is the right ingredient for the team.

We must remember this truth: it only takes one rotten apple to spoil the bunch. The harder question we avoid is this: Did we bring that apple into the bunch ourselves?

Introducing a new team member who does not align with the culture is like buying whole milk when the entire household lactose intolerant. You can't force the fit. Tension follows when the dynamic is off. Resources will be drained. Energy will shift away from growth and toward conflict. The wrong ingredient does not just affect itself; it impacts everything in the pot.

And once that happens, a stall-out can occur.

After all, most leaders find hiring easier than releasing. While it is true that it takes time to search for the right ingredients, throwing something out once it has expired is not easy. It might seem simpler, but we forget the fact that emotional attachment is involved. When someone is hurting the team, creating daily tension, failing to meet expectations, or causing organizational pain, it is time to act. This is never simple. And it should never be. But stewarding the role of leadership well means we must embrace hard conversations and tough choices.

Releasing someone from a role should never stem from a quick trigger moment, done out of anger or heightened emotion. Before removing anyone from your team, you must ask hard questions: Have I truly done everything possible to develop this person? Did I place them in the right position to succeed, or did I set them up to fail? Could they have thrived in a different role, a different lane, or with clearer expectations? One of the least discussed topics at leadership conferences is termination, yet it is one of the most defining moments of leadership.

I did not truly understand how to let someone go until I faced this duty early in my leadership journey. I remember sitting there with sweaty palms, nervous, unsure, and questioning myself.

I kept asking: Am I making the best decision for the team, or am I making the easiest decision for me? That question matters because those two answers are not always the same.

Some leaders confuse personal discomfort with poor performance. They remove strong employees simply because of personality conflict or avoidance. That is not leadership; that is self-protection.

But when an employee consistently damages morale, impedes progress, resists growth, or exhausts the team despite coaching, improvement plans, and support, the responsibility shifts. At that point, the decision is no longer about preference; it is about stewardship.

A good leader always prioritizes what is best for the team over what is most comfortable for themselves. Because of this, a level of sacrifice is required. And yet, letting someone go is never easy. You are impacting a family. You are breaking a routine. You are closing a chapter you once believed in. If a leader ever tells you that termination is easy, that should concern you. It means they never truly invested in their people.

This is where the **THANKFUL Method** must guide every decision, not just who you bring in, but how you steward those already in the kitchen. Transparency sets expectations early. Humility keeps leaders from hiring in their own image. Adaptability allows space for growth. Nurturing commits to development before judgment. Kneeling keeps the process covered in prayer. Faithfulness ensures consistency. Unity protects culture. Loyalty sustains trust, even in hard conversations.

**Going shopping is not a sign of instability.
It is a sign of stewardship.**

Wise leaders understand that timing matters, seasons change, and courage is required to act when something no longer serves the mission.

Leaders who refuse to shop eventually end up cooking with expired ingredients, and the cost is always paid by the team. Leaders who shop wisely build meals that nourish everyone at the table, even when the process is uncomfortable.

So, take your time. Check the labels. Inspect what you select. Ask the hard questions. Pray before you decide. The people you invite into your kitchen, and the decisions you make when seasons shift, shape your culture long after the interview ends. Leadership is not about filling positions. It is about stewarding people, purpose, and trust in a way that allows the entire organization to thrive.

Reflection and Discussion:

We steward our leadership best when we allow time for decision-making. Therefore, it is important for us to reflect on how we make choices and on the internal obstacles we face when finding the right ingredients.

To help us take an internal stock of our decision-making style, consider the following questions and discussion prompts.

For Leaders and Hiring Teams:

1. What ingredients on my current team are thriving, and which may need renewal, development, or repositioning?

2. Have I clearly defined the cultural "flavor" we are trying to protect and multiply?

3. Where might I be tolerating misalignment because it is uncomfortable to address?

4. Am I hiring or promoting based on character and alignment with the **THANKFUL Method**, or simply based on skill and urgency?

5. When was the last time I truly "shopped intentionally" instead of hiring quickly?

6. Have I prayed over any current hiring decision, or am I rushing to fill a gap?

7. What qualities does our team need next, not just right now?

Team Discussion:

1. What does it look like for our team to shop wisely rather than shop quickly?

2. Which **THANKFUL** ingredient best represents our current culture? Which one needs strengthening?

3. How can we better align our hiring practices with our values?

4. What responsibility do we have to prepare new hires to perform and grow into future leaders?

5. How can we protect unity and trust during seasons of transition?

Hiring Discernment Checklist

The **THANKFUL Method** Applied to Hiring:

Before placing a new ingredient into the pot, every chef pauses to inspect it closely. Similarly, hiring is not about filling space. It is about protecting the integrity of the team's dynamic.

To help us make wise choices in our hiring processes, consider asking the following questions to assess a candidate's quality and culture-fit. Note that this list is not meant to replace intuition or prayer, but to sharpen decision-making.

Transparent

Have we clearly communicated our organization's expectations from the beginning? And did the candidate respond well? If so, what indicators of alignment were present?

Does this candidate speak honestly about strengths, weaknesses, and past challenges?

Can this candidate articulate failure without blame or excuses?

Humble

Does this person show teachability, or do they carry themselves as if they have nothing left to learn?

How do they speak regarding their former supervisors and teams?
Do they honor others without elevating themselves? If so, what indicators were present?

Adaptable

How has the candidate responded to changes in their past roles?

Can they describe a moment when they had to pivot without becoming defensive or disengaged?

What did you note that makes you believe they are flexible without compromising values?

Nurturer

Does the candidate invest in people, or only in tasks? What indicators suggest they lean toward one or the other?

How do they respond to underperformance in others?

Do they see team development as an inconvenience or a responsibility?

Kneeler

Is there evidence of prayer, reflection, or dependence on something greater than themselves?

Do they acknowledge the limits of their own strength and wisdom?

Do they make decisions with discernment or impulse? What indicators suggest they lean toward one or the other?

Faithful

Is there consistency between what the candidate says and what they have done?

Do their work history and relationships reflect commitment and endurance? If so, what did you perceive about them regarding these attributes?

Are they steady when things become difficult? What leads you to say yes or no?

Unifier

How does the candidate handle conflict?

Do they build bridges or take sides? What indicators suggest they lean toward one or the other?

Are they capable of bringing people together when tensions are high? If so, what did you perceive about them regarding their ability to do so?

Loyal

How has the candidate demonstrated respect for mission even when their leadership changed?

Do they protect the team or center themselves? What indicators suggest they lean toward one or the other?

Is loyalty shown through action rather than words? If so, what did you perceive about them regarding this skill?

As you reflect on your perception of the candidate, along with their answers, consider the fact that if multiple ingredients raise concern, this is not hesitation. That is wisdom.

Leadership Action Step

Taking time to consider your personal hiring practices and how your team approaches building a team, I invite you to build a plan to ensure you have the right ingredients.

Before your next hire, commit to this practice:

Pause.
Pray.
Inspect the ingredients.

Do not ask only if someone can do the job. Ask if they will enhance the meal.

When the Kitchen Loses Its Purpose

A kitchen doesn't lose its purpose when it runs out of ingredients, it loses its purpose when it forgets what it's meant to serve. You can have every ingredient in place, every tool within reach, and still produce something that looks right but fails to nourish. Because purpose is not found in what's available, it's found in what's intended.

Purpose rarely disappears all at once. It fades like a dish slowly losing its flavor. Not because leaders stop caring, but because something begins to shift beneath the surface. What once drove the mission slowly gets replaced, sometimes by comparison, sometimes by control, and sometimes by the quiet desire to be seen.

At first, nothing feels different. The kitchen is still active. The work is still being done. From the outside, everything appears intact.

But something has changed.

The same ingredients may be present, but something is off. The balance is gone. The taste is different.

What once nourished people now feels empty. What once brought unity now creates tension. What once served others begins, little by little, to serve self. Every leader will face moments where purpose is tested. Sometimes it comes through external pressure. Sometimes it rises internally through disappointment, comparison, or unmet expectations.

The danger is not the moment itself. The danger is what happens when that shift goes unexamined.

Leaders who are not grounded in a framework like the **THANKFUL Method** can begin making decisions from misalignment instead of mission. Instead of leading with humility, transparency, and faithfulness, they begin leading from pressure, perception, and control.

And when that happens, the kitchen does not shut down. It just stops producing what it was created for. Leadership has a way of revealing what is happening beneath the surface, if you are willing to pay attention. One of the most subtle shifts a leader can experience is the movement from purpose to position.

It doesn't happen all at once. It begins when attention shifts from impact to recognition.

When awareness turns into comparison. When responsibility starts to feel like ownership.

And in that moment, something begins to drift.

What once fueled the mission slowly becomes replaced by something else. Not always visible. Not always intentional. But real. It's like following a recipe but ignoring the timing, the heat, and the order of ingredients. Everything is still there, but the outcome no longer nourishes.

And when that drift goes unchecked, the kitchen may still be active, but it is no longer aligned.

Too many leaders allow disappointment to harden them. They get burned once, and instead of healing, they build armor. Slowly, their focus shifts. Their heart changes. They become someone they never intended to be, not because they lacked talent, but because they never processed the hurt. Leadership does not just test your ability; it tests your heart.

Leadership often reveals itself not in boardrooms or titles, but in the quiet moments we are tempted to walk past. It shows up in what catches our attention, in what troubles us enough to linger, and in what we choose to carry once we notice it. Every leader will encounter moments where awareness demands action, where seeing becomes responsibility. These moments test more than skill; they test stewardship. They expose whether our leadership is driven by recognition or rooted in care, shaped by comparison, or anchored in purpose. What we do with what we see will determine whether our leadership nourishes others or slowly becomes about us.

I learned this lesson through an experience that began quietly. When my daughter started kindergarten, I walked her to class on the first day like any proud parent would. As I stood there, I noticed two children who reminded me of myself at that age. They had no backpacks. No school supplies. No fresh haircut. Not because their families did not care, but because they did not have the means.

115

When I shared what I saw with my wife, she asked a simple but unsettling question. What are you going to do about it? That question demanded action, not emotion. It demanded leadership. I remembered something a supervisor once told me. If there is one, there are others. That mindset moved us beyond sympathy and into responsibility.

Our family decided to start a backpack initiative for children in our hometown. We had no budget and no formal plan. What we had was conviction. Our church committed first. My workplace opened its campus. Volunteers stepped forward. Barbers donated their time. What began as a small act of care quickly grew into something far larger than we imagined.

On the morning of the event, families arrived before the sun came up. By mid-morning, hundreds were waiting in line. When the doors opened, the need was overwhelming. We distributed five hundred backpacks in less than an hour. We ran out of food. We ran out of supplies. But we did not run out of heart.

At one point, our personal bank account hit zero from trying to get extra that was still needed. We still had volunteers to feed and children to serve. We trusted the moment and kept going. That is kneeling leadership and faith in motion. It is not comfortable. It is not convenient. But it is right.

Over the years, the event grew into the largest backpack giveaway in our county. Thousands of children were served annually. Families were supported. Community was restored. It was never about recognition. It was about responsibility. But success has a way of attracting attention. And attention, if not grounded in purpose, can begin to shift focus.

Eventually, the event was taken over by others. Shortly after, it failed.

Children lost resources.
Families lost support.
A community lost something that once nourished it.

Because when the wrong ingredients are introduced, or the right ones are mishandled, the meal may still be served, but it no longer sustains. That is what happens when purpose is replaced by position.

It does not just affect one person.

It spreads.
It fractures trust.
It leaves gaps that are difficult to restore.

When that happened, I was hurt. Not mildly disappointed. Not professionally frustrated. Hurt.

I wanted to defend what was built.
I wanted to explain the heart behind it.
I wanted to protect the families it was created for.

For the life of me, I could not understand how something rooted in service could be redirected into something centered on visibility.

And if I am honest, something began forming inside of me.

- Resentment
- Disbelief
- A quiet frustration that did not feel like me

I replayed conversations.
I rehearsed responses.
I imagined explanations I would never give.

It was as if something bitter had entered my spirit, and if I wasn't careful, it would change the way I showed up in every room.

That is what unprocessed hurt does. It keeps the moment alive long after it has passed.

But underneath all of that was something deeper.
I was grieving.

Not just the loss of the program.
Not just the loss of trust.
I was grieving the loss of something sacred.

My wife looked me in the eyes and said, "Let it go."
My pastor said, "It's okay."
My children said, "We can do something else."

They were not dismissing the pain. They were protecting my heart.

Because what we often fail to recognize is this:

The same misalignment we see in others can begin forming in us. Hurt does not only distort those who take. It can begin to reshape those who feel wronged.

And if left unaddressed, it will change how you lead

Recognizing the Shift Within Yourself

Misalignment is not always obvious. Sometimes it sounds like justification.

- "They ruined what we built."
- "They don't deserve it."
- "They wouldn't even have this without us."

These thoughts feel valid.

But left unchecked, they begin to season your leadership in ways you never intended.

You may notice:

- You struggle to celebrate what once brought you joy
- You replay conversations more than you pursue healing
- You measure influence instead of impact
- You feel the need to remind others of your role
- You begin protecting your position instead of the purpose

This is how drift happens.

Not all at once.
But over time.

I came to a realization I could not ignore:

If I allowed that hurt to remain, it would contaminate the very ingredients that started this work in the first place.

And that is when the **THANKFUL Method** became more than a framework.

It became a decision.

Leadership rooted in the **THANKFUL Method** does not ignore pain. It processes it.

Transparency forced me to admit I was hurt.

Humility reminded me it was never mine to own.

Adaptability challenged me to release what had changed.

Nurturing called me to protect my heart.

Kneeling brought me back to prayer when pride wanted a voice.

Faithfulness reminded me that obedience matters more than recognition.

Unity told me not to fracture what remained.

Loyalty called me to stay aligned with purpose, not position. Because leadership is not just about having the right ingredients, it is about protecting them.

I chose alignment.

Not because it was easy.
Not because it felt fair.
But because it was necessary.

And here is the truth: letting go was harder than launching.

Every leader is responsible for what they bring into the kitchen and what they allow to remain.

Leadership always involves sacrifice. There will be moments when things do not go as planned. Effort will not always be recognized. Outcomes will not always reflect the heart behind the work.

But there is a difference between a difficult season and a distorted purpose. When leaders lose sight of purpose, everything changes.

Organizations shift from impact to image.

Teams move from collaboration to competition.

Communities feel the absence of something they cannot always explain, but deeply recognize.

Because when the kitchen loses its purpose, it may still produce something, but it no longer nourishes.

That is why the **THANKFUL Method** matters.

Transparent leaders confront misalignment early.
Humble leaders remember it was never theirs to own.
Adaptable leaders release what has changed.
Nurturing leaders protect people over platforms.
Kneeling leaders surrender control in prayer.

Faithful leaders stay committed when recognition fades.
Unified leaders guard what remains.
Loyal leaders stay aligned with purpose, not position.

Leadership that kneels does not need to compete.
Leadership that serves does not need to control.
Leadership rooted in the **THANKFUL Method** does not chase recognition. It protects nourishment.

The question every leader must answer is simple. Are you here to be seen or to serve? The answer will determine whether what you are building feeds people or leaves them hungry

Reflection Questions

1. Where in my leadership has the "flavor" of my purpose started to change?

2. When have I shifted from serving the mission to protecting my position?

3. What hurt or disappointment have I left unprocessed that may be affecting how I lead?

4. Where have I focused more on recognition than responsibility?

5. What am I holding onto that I may need to release in order to realign with purpose?

6. In what ways might I be adding the wrong "ingredients" into my leadership environment?

Team Discussion Guide

For Leadership Teams

- Where do we see signs that our team is drifting from purpose to position?

- What behaviors suggest we are protecting roles instead of serving the mission?

- How do we ensure the "ingredients" we bring into this team environment are healthy and aligned?

- Where might unspoken hurt or tension be affecting how we lead and collaborate?

- What would it look like for us to realign our leadership with transparency, humility, and unity?

- How do we protect the purpose of our team as we grow and gain visibility?

For Organizations

- Do our systems reinforce purpose, or do they unintentionally reward position and visibility?

- Where have we seen mission drift, even if results still look successful?

- How do we measure whether our leadership is truly nourishing people, not just producing outcomes?

- What structures or habits help us stay aligned
  with our original purpose?

- Where do we need to reintroduce the right
  "ingredients" into our culture?

- Which **THANKFUL** principle is currently weakest
  in our organization, and how is that affecting our
  impact?

Stay In The Kitchen

My wife and I went to dinner one night, and as we drove the fifteen minutes to the restaurant, I did what many leaders do. I vented. I talked about my day at work, the goals still unfinished, the deadlines looming, the items still outstanding. My mind was full and my stomach was empty and I couldn't wait to finally park our car.

As we stepped out and walked toward the entrance, the front doors of the restaurant flung open. The head chef and the manager were arguing in full view of everyone. The chef was exhausted. He said he could not take it anymore. Long hours. The kitchen was short-staffed. Plates were being dropped. Meals were being sent back. Only two others were in the kitchen with him and he could not take it anymore. He finally said, "You can have this job. I'm done," and sat down on the floor.

The manager did not raise his voice. He did not threaten him. He walked over, got down to the chef's level, looked him in the eye, and said eight simple words. "Can you please go back to the kitchen?"

In that moment, the kitchen stopped being about food, it became about posture. Because when a leader is willing to lower themselves, to meet someone at eye level instead of standing over them, something shifts. It's like stepping off your feet and onto the floor, not to lose authority, but to restore alignment. Because real leadership isn't proven by how high you stand, but by how low you're willing to go to bring someone back to where they belong.

Leadership will bring you to moments like that. You will face moments when you are tired, overwhelmed, frustrated, and ready to walk away. Moments when quitting feels justified. But we were built for these moments. Leadership is not about avoiding the burden. It is about carrying it when it is heavy.

**Quitting is easy.
Leading is hard**.

I often say leadership is great when everything is working. But what happens when everything stinks, and you have to stand in it? That is real leadership. That is staying in the kitchen when the heat is turned up and the pressure is high.

The chef was not weak. He was human. He had given everything he had and finally hit a breaking point. And here is the lesson. It is okay to pause. It is okay to step away for a moment. It is okay to cry, yell, breathe, and collect yourself. What is not okay is becoming a quitter. If you quit once, quitting becomes an option again and again. Leaders must learn how to recover without retreating.

There is something dangerous about walking out of the kitchen.

It's like leaving a stove unattended with the heat still on. The food doesn't stop cooking just because you stepped away. It begins to burn. The flavors break down. What once had the potential to nourish can quickly become something no one can consume. And the longer it's left unattended, the harder it is to recover what was lost.

When a leader checks out emotionally, even if they are still physically present, the temperature in the room changes. Conversations become shorter. Patience thins. Vision blurs. People can feel it long before you ever say it.

The kitchen does not only represent a job. It represents responsibility.

And responsibility is rarely glamorous.

There are days when the orders keep coming, and no one thanks you for the meal. There are seasons when you are short-staffed, under-resourced, and overextended. There are moments when the very people you are serving send the plate back.

That is when quitting whispers:

"You deserve better."
"No one appreciates you."
"This isn't worth it."

The whisper sounds rational. Logical. Even justified.

But leadership maturity is measured by what you do when quitting makes sense.

Staying in the kitchen is not stubbornness. It is stewardship. It understands that what you are building is bigger than how you feel in the moment.

This lesson became personal for me during my son's junior year of high school. After two years of disciplined training, proper nutrition, and countless hours in the gym, he made it to the state championship in weightlifting. He had placed first in nearly every meet leading up to that day. Family and friends filled the bleachers. The moment had arrived.

On his first attempt, he scratched.

As his father, I saw it immediately. The look in his eyes took me back to when he was eight or nine years old. Fear. Disappointment. Overwhelm. There on the mat, a tear rolled down his face. I ran to the floor. He broke down. The lights were too bright. The moment felt too big.

I grabbed his chin, lifted his face, and said, "Son, we have worked for this moment for two years. It is okay to scratch your first lift. But it is not okay to quit."

He had the right ingredients. He had just lost his faith in the process. He regrouped, finished strong, and placed in the top ten.

As I watched my son regroup, I realized something powerful. Pressure does not create character. It reveals it. In that moment, he did not need a new training plan. He did not need a different coach. He did not need the crowd to quiet down. He needed perspective.

Leaders often lose perspective before they lose strength. We begin focusing on the scratch instead of the total body of work. We magnify one mistake until it overshadows years of preparation. We let one bad meeting define an entire plan.

The state championship did not expose my son's weakness. It exposed the moment he needed encouragement. And that is what leaders need too.

Not constant praise.
Not unrealistic expectations.

But someone who will look them in the eyes and say, "It is not okay to quit."

If you do not have someone who can speak that into you, you are more vulnerable than you think. Every leader needs a voice that pulls them back into the kitchen.

My son's tournament reminded me of something critical. Leadership does not start at work. It starts at home. If I could encourage excellence in a boardroom but not resilience in my own son, I had failed. The most important leadership moments rarely come with applause. They come in private, uncomfortable spaces where someone needs you to help them stay in the kitchen.

My wife has reminded me of this more than once. She has told me, "I need the leader you are at work. I need that same man here." What she was really saying was this. Do not spend all your best ingredients at work and leave scraps at home.

Leadership is like cooking. Work may be the main dish everyone sees, but home is the base ingredient. If the foundation is weak, the entire meal suffers. You can season a dish perfectly, but if the base is spoiled, the flavor will never be right. A leader who pours all their energy into work and neglects home eventually burns out, grows bitter, or loses perspective.

Home leadership is where accountability begins. It is where blind spots are exposed. It is where someone loves you enough to tell you the truth. That kind of accountability protects you from burnout long before it shows up at work.

There is another side to this metaphor that we rarely discuss. Some leaders stay in the corporate kitchen but abandon the one at home. They endure pressure at work, absorb conflict, solve problems, and manage personalities all day long. Then they walk through their front door with nothing left to give. They give their employer their best ingredients. They give their family the leftovers. And slowly, the base ingredient spoils.

The truth is, you can succeed publicly and fail privately.

You can build teams and lose connection with your spouse.
You can mentor employees and neglect your children.
You can manage crises at work and ignore tension at home.

But here is what few will tell you:

If your home kitchen collapses, eventually everything else will taste bitter. Home is not a distraction from leadership. It is the proving ground of it. If you cannot stay patient in your living room, your patience in the boardroom is mere performance. If you cannot lead with integrity in private, your public leadership will crack.

Staying in the kitchen begins at home because that is where your leadership is tested without applause.

Your journey will require a pick-me-up from time to time. There will be seasons when you feel empty. When your strength is gone and fatigue sets in. In those moments, you must rely on strength greater than your own. The same way my son needed a voice to pull him back into focus, and the chef needed someone to meet him at his lowest point, leaders need people who will remind them who they are and why they started.

Staying in the kitchen does not mean ignoring rest. It means knowing when to pause without abandoning your post. Take the vacation. Spend time with your family. Care for your mental health. Do it before burnout turns into bitterness and exhaustion turns into depression.

Staying in the kitchen does not mean staying exhausted. It means staying faithful.

It means knowing when to rest without resigning. It means pausing without abandoning your post. It means protecting your home with the same intensity you protect your career.

**Leadership is not proven
when the heat is low.**

It is proven when the burners are all on, and the orders keep coming.

There will be days when you feel like the chef on the floor.

There will be moments when you feel like my son under the lights.

There will be seasons when your strength feels spent.

Pause.
Breathe.
Kneel.

But do not quit.

Because the people at your table are depending on what you are preparing.

Stay in the kitchen!

Your family needs you there first.

And when the kitchen at home is healthy, every meal you serve everywhere else will carry the right flavor.

Reflection and Discussion Questions

Personal Reflection

1. When I look honestly at my life, where do I give my best ingredients, at work or at home?

2. What ingredients am I unintentionally bringing home at the end of the day, patience or leftovers, presence or exhaustion?

3. Have I ever justified neglect at home by calling it a sacrifice for work?

4. What warning signs tell me I am close to quitting internally, even if I am still showing up externally?

5. Who in my life has permission to tell me when I am burning out or misplacing my priorities?

Leadership at Home

6. How does my leadership at home shape my leadership at work?

7. If my family were to describe my leadership, what words would they use?

8. What would change in my household if I invested the same intentionality at home that I do in my profession?

9. Am I modeling perseverance at home or only performing it publicly?

Food and Ingredient Alignment

10.   Which ingredient do I reserve only for work that my family actually needs more of?

11.   Where have I substituted cheap ingredients at home, short answers, distractions, or emotional absence?

12.   What does it look like to prepare a nourishing meal for my family, not just a functional one?

Commitment and Action

13.   What is one boundary I need to set to protect my family's seat at the table?

14.   What is one practice that would help me stay in the kitchen without burning out?

15.   What does staying in the kitchen look like in this season faithfully?

Setting The Table

Timing is everything. There is nothing like knowing the meal you have been preparing is almost finished. The hard work of planning, the patience of gathering the right ingredients, and the discipline of staying present through the process have each brought you to this moment. The aroma of excellence now fills the room, reaching farther than you ever expected.

And now, it is time to set the table.

This is the moment when you prepare to receive what you sacrificed so much to create.

A mentor of mine once told me, "If you don't have a seat at the table, then you are on the menu." At the time, I laughed, but his words stayed with me. It was more than a clever phrase; it was a warning. It spoke to power, influence, and presence. It reminded me that decisions are always being made somewhere, and if you are not present, you may be affected without ever being heard.

That statement created a hunger in me. I pushed myself to grow, to lead well, to show up prepared so that when a seat opened, I was ready to sit down. I wanted to ensure that my team had a voice, that their work was represented, and that their sacrifices were not overlooked. I believed that having a seat meant security, influence, and impact.

What I eventually learned, however, is that leadership does not end once you sit down. In fact, sometimes the real work begins there. Because even when you earn a seat at one table, there is often another table you didn't even know existed, one where deeper decisions are made, values are tested, and character matters more than credentials.

The first time I sat at a table I had prayed and prepared for, I thought I had arrived. I was finally included in a high-level meeting. Decisions were being made that would impact teams, budgets, and direction for years to come. I had prepared. I had notes. I had thoughts I believed needed to be heard.

And then something unexpected happened. I realized that having a seat does not automatically mean having influence. There were conversations happening beneath the conversation. History I did not know. Relationships I did not understand. Agendas I could not see.

That is when I learned a hard truth:

You can speak too early and lose credibility.
You can speak too often and lose weight.
You can speak emotionally and lose trust.

Being at the table is not about dominating the discussion. It is about discerning contribution. Some leaders sit down and immediately start rearranging plates that were already positioned intentionally. Others remain silent out of fear and never add value at all. Mature leadership knows when to adjust the silverware and when to leave it alone. Influence is earned through restraint as much as through voice.

Leadership is not just about access; it's about stewardship. It's about knowing when to speak, when to listen, and when to protect what is being built. Not every table requires your voice, and not every recipe needs your opinion. Wisdom teaches us how to discern the difference.

My wife's grandfather understood the power of stewarding a rich history well. He was an incredible man from Louisiana with an unbelievable gift for cooking. He didn't use measuring cups or written recipes. He cooked from memory, instinct, taste, and timing. Every meal carried history. Every dish told a story.

I loved his food so much that one day I asked him, "Granddad, can you show me how to make your étouffée?" He looked at me, smiled, and said, "Huh… but you're not from Louisiana." We both laughed, but in that moment, I realized something crucial. He was guarding his recipe. Not out of selfishness, but out of stewardship.

That moment with Granddad stayed with me longer than the joke. He was not protecting the recipe out of insecurity. He was protecting it because it carried legacy. Some tables require open recipes. Others require guarded wisdom.

Not every room deserves full access to your convictions. Not every platform deserves your raw emotion. Not every opportunity deserves your endorsement. When leaders over-share, they weaken the dish. When leaders withhold out of fear, they starve the table. Wisdom sits in between.

There are conversations that belong in private kitchens, not public dining rooms. There are corrections that must happen before the meal is served. There are strategies that must mature before they are announced.

Therefore, setting the table is about protecting what is still cooking.

That is stewardship.

As leaders, there are things we cannot share with everyone. Not every thought needs to be spoken. Not every concern needs to be voiced immediately. Emotional leadership or reacting to everything we feel or hear can ruin the meal before it ever reaches the table. Wisdom knows what to release and what to protect.

I often tell my leadership team, "I cannot be the boss and be uncomfortable." What I mean is this: we cannot come to work every day with unresolved issues, unspoken tension, and broken trust. That environment doesn't work, and it never will. In leadership, I would rather take distance over disrespect.

Sometimes stepping back prevents a situation from boiling over. It protects relationships that might otherwise be damaged for weeks, months, or even permanently.

Leadership requires maturity to pause, reflect, and respond rather than react.

Setting the table matters. The fork, spoon, and knife all have a place. The plate must be centered. The glass must be clean and ready. Leadership is the same way. It's about placing the right people in the right seats at the right time.

If you sit down to eat and everything is out of order, the fork is misplaced, the wrong glass is grabbed, it throws off the entire experience. First impressions matter. First interactions matter. They set the tone for everything that follows.

I've noticed that people often value a title more than they value the person. That realization changed how I show up. Over the last few years, I stopped leading with my title during introductions unless I was asked. I noticed that once people believed you held status, they treated you differently. But leadership is not about status; it's about service.

I am no more important than the maintenance worker, the landscaper, or the person quietly keeping things running behind the scenes. If the title doesn't match the heart, then something is broken.

Titles can secure a seat, but character determines whether you keep it. I have seen leaders fight aggressively to be invited into rooms, only to mishandle the moment once they arrived. They spoke over others. They dismissed quieter voices. They confused authority with superiority. That behavior unsettles the table.

The strongest leaders I have observed are not the loudest in the room. They ask thoughtful questions. They draw out wisdom from others. They protect people who are not present to defend themselves. They do not treat the table as a stage. They treat it as a responsibility.

When you sit down, remember this: Someone sacrificed for you to be there.

Your mentors sacrificed.
Your family sacrificed.
Your team sacrificed.

Setting the table well honors them.

This is where the **THANKFUL Method** becomes critical. It forces reflection. It reveals misalignment. It calls leaders back to humility, transparency, and purpose. When the heart matches the title, the table is set correctly.

I'll be the first to admit that I've failed in setting tables. I've dropped forks. I've spilled drinks. I've eaten dessert before the meal. But I learned. Every fork can be washed. Every spill can be cleaned. Every mistake can become an instruction if you're willing to learn.

Leadership feels hard because it requires patience. We rush. We grab stained tablecloths because we're in a hurry. We build teams quickly only to realize months later that the foundation is cracked. It's always better to slow down and set the table correctly than to rush and start over.

There is another dimension to setting the table that we rarely discuss. Sometimes you must decide who does not belong at it. That decision is not rooted in ego. It is rooted in alignment.

If someone continually disrespects the culture, undermines trust, or poisons conversation, leaving them at the table damages everyone else who is trying to eat. That is not exclusion, but it's protection.

Every table has a standard.
Every kitchen has a code.

If you compromise values just to fill seats, the meal will suffer. Leadership requires courage to protect the table from what would quietly destroy it. That courage is not loud. It is consistent.

As you move forward in leadership, don't crush what hasn't had time to bloom. Water it. Protect it. Position it for success. Take time to prepare well so the mission can flourish.

Not every table will look the same. Not every seat will be filled by the same people. But when you finally sit down, take time to engage with those around you. Listen. Learn. Build relationships. You never know who you'll work for, work with, or learn from in the future.

Leadership has the power to make even the smallest table a model for others. When it's set with care, humility, and intention, people notice.

In the end, leadership is not about fighting for a chair. It is about preparing a place where others can flourish.

It is about setting the table with intention, aligning the right people, protecting the culture, honoring the mission, and serving with humility once everyone is seated.

When you earn a seat, do not waste it.
When you prepare a table, do not rush it.
When you serve the meal, do not make it about yourself.

One day, your name will be removed from the table, but your influence will remain in every seat.

They won't remember your position, but they will feel your presence in the way things are done. In the way people are treated. In the way the meal is served.

Because what you prepare outlives you.

So set the table well not for recognition, but for legacy. Because the meal was never meant to end with you. It was always about who it would feed next.

Reflection and Discussion Guide

Setting the Table: Seats, Recipes, and Responsibility

Personal Reflection

1. When you hear the phrase "If you don't have a seat at the table, you are on the menu," what emotions does it stir in you? Do you sense fear, motivation, insecurity, clarity, or something else? Why?

2. Where in your leadership journey have you chased a seat at the table more than you chased responsibility for those already within your care?

3. Have you ever discovered there was another table, a decision-making space or influence circle, you didn't know existed? How did that realization change you?

4. What "recipes" in your leadership do you guard closely? Which ones are rooted in wisdom, and which may be rooted in control or fear?

5. Are there moments when you speak too openly with the wrong audience, or remain too silent with the right one? What discernment is missing?

6. When tension rises, do you tend to choose distance or discomfort? How has that choice impacted your relationships long-term?

7.   Do you believe your heart currently matches the responsibilities found deep within your title? Why or why not?

Leadership Practice & Awareness

8.   How intentional are you about who sits where on your team? Are people positioned by calling and capability or by convenience?

9.   In what ways might you be using a "stained tablecloth" from the past, old habits, unresolved conflict, outdated assumptions, to set a new table?

10.   Have you ever moved too quickly in building a team or initiative, only to realize later that the foundation was cracked? What did it cost you?

11.   How do you handle first impressions and introductions? Do you lead with title, function, or presence?

12.   When was the last time you intentionally honored someone at the table who had no formal authority?

13.   What systems or rhythms help you to ensure that your forks, spoons, and knives are in the right place before the meal begins?

It's Time To Eat

As a child, I remember my mother working in the kitchen for hours, preparing meals with patience and purpose. No matter what dish she was making, she always kept a wooden spoon close by. Every so often, she would call me over and offer a small taste. That moment was not the finished product, but a glimpse of what was coming. She wanted me to understand the flavors along the way, not just the result.

When the meal was finally ready, she would raise her voice and call across the house, "It's time to eat." Everything stopped. We gathered and sat at a table that had been prepared for us. We arrived ready to receive what had been cooked with intention. What we tasted in that moment was more than food. It was time, sacrifice, and love made visible.

She stayed in that kitchen for hours, not because she had to, but because she loved to. No matter how hot it became, she wiped the sweat from her face and kept going.

What you prepare for others will always carry the condition of your heart.

When utensils fell, she washed them and continued. When an ingredient ran out, she went back to the store and returned without complaint. She never abandoned the process because it became uncomfortable.

Leadership requires that same understanding. If we are going to accept this calling, we must love the work, not just the outcome. We must value the process that leads to meaningful outcomes. Getting to the point where you can partake in that meal demands long hours, dropped dishes, fatigue, and resilience. There will be moments when you sit down only to realize you must stand back up and return to the kitchen. But if you stay faithful to the process, one day you will look around the table and realize the work was worth it.

Every leader learns this truth eventually. For me, I learned it at home. Long before I understood leadership frameworks, organizational culture, or sacrifice, I watched leadership lived out in my mother's kitchen. It was not a place for speeches or strategy, but it brimmed to the surface in consistency, patience, and love. My parents' home is where I first learned what it meant to stay with the process until the meal was ready.

And yet, leadership is never without testing.

146

I remember a project I poured myself into, thinking I had done everything right. Supplies were missing. Volunteers didn't show. Chaos threatened to undo everything we had worked for. I could have walked away, blamed others, or shrugged. Instead, I stayed in the kitchen. I improvised. I encouraged my team. I focused on what mattered most. When the dust settled, the meal was served, and the impact exceeded anything I could have predicted. That moment reminded me that leadership is not about avoiding chaos; it's about guiding through it without losing sight of the purpose.

When everything is ready, you will know it. The kitchen will be quiet. The knives will have been set down. The heat has been adjusted. The ingredients have been measured, cut, seasoned, and patiently prepared. What once felt chaotic has become intentional. This is the moment every leader works toward, whether they realize it or not. This is where preparation leads us to purpose.

You can smell the work in the air. You can feel the weight of what it took to get here. Nothing on the table is accidental. Every choice, correction, and pause mattered. Now, something truly wonderful is in front of you, and it's time to eat.

This meal carries a story. It reflects the times you were cut but kept going. It represents the seasons when you had to go shopping because what you had wasn't enough. It speaks to the moments when contamination tried to poison the kitchen, but you remained diligent in protecting the mission. The fact that you are here reminds you of the nights you wanted to walk out but chose instead to stay in the kitchen.

Every plate we serve, every team we lead, every mentee we pour into, these are prepared through the ingredients of the **THANKFUL Method**. Transparency ensures honesty in taste; humility allows the recipe to be corrected; adaptability handles unexpected substitutions; nurturing protects the final meal. Kneeling in prayer, faithfulness, unity, and loyalty season every choice. Leadership lived this way produces meals that are worth remembering.

This plate holds the evidence of leadership lived with intention, measured, patient, **THANKFUL**. Some flavors are bold. Others are subtle. All of them belong. What you are about to consume was shaped not just by skill, but by sacrifice.

But eating is not the end of the work, it is the reveal. We are past preparation, position, or potential. Now, we live the story. The table tells that story honestly. If the ingredients were rushed, the taste would show it. If ego replaced humility, the bitterness would linger. If faith, faithfulness, and care have guided the process, nourishment will follow.

The shared meal is where leaders find out if they cooked to impress or cooked to serve.

In leadership, we often extend ourselves to others with the hope of building what comes next. I once had a mentor tell me, "I'm going to retire soon, and I need to make sure I pour into someone who will take care of the people." What he meant was this: I didn't spend thirty-plus years building something just to watch it collapse under the weight of an ill-equipped, ego-driven leader. Because leadership is not about building something while you are present. Its about building something that still nourishes people when you are gone.

Mentorship matters because people matter. Leadership is stewardship, and legacy does not happen by accident.

At some point, every leader realizes the kitchen is no longer just a place they visit; it is a place they own. The apron fits differently when someone is watching you cook. Here, decisions linger longer. When legacy is on the line, your tone, patience, and faith season more than just the work in front of you.

Whether you asked for it or not, someone is learning how to lead by watching you. They are curious how you will respond when the heat rises. They will pay attention to how you recover when something burns.

Leadership does not announce this truth; it simply reveals it *quietly*. And once you recognize the level of influence you carry, you cannot pretend you are just a helper anymore.

You are the cook now.

Before you close the chapter, pause. Take a deep breath. Consider the meals you've prepared for others. Reflect on your teams, your mentees, your family, and your community. Which dishes were seasoned with intention? Which could have used more care? Gratitude surfaces here, for lessons learned, for scars that taught compassion, and or opportunities to serve when it wasn't convenient.

Now, you get to decide what comes next. Which ingredients will you prioritize? Which recipes need attention? How would someone rate your leadership menu? Leadership is a continual kitchen. The work does not end, even after the table is full. Every choice matters. Every interaction leaves a flavor behind.

Leadership always leaves a taste behind. Families carry it home. Teams talk about it when you are not in the room. The way you handle pressure, conflict, disappointment, and growth becomes part of someone else's story. That is why the process matters so much. But you know this. You understand stewardship. It is why you stayed in the kitchen, even though it would have been easier to walk out.

Therefore, I invite you to pause.

Take a moment to draw one deep, long breath in and out. Think about the meal you are preparing for others. And before the final call is made and the table fills, stand still to review what you have laid out for others. Look at what you have prepared, not with pride, but with gratitude. Go back to the roots of thankfulness for lessons that cost you something. Let gratitude surface, even for the scars. Reflect with a **THANKFUL** heart that you have faith, which carried you when skill alone was not enough.

After all, your leadership journey was never about perfection. It was always about posture. A posture of humility, stewardship, faithfulness, and care. If you can continue in that posture, this meal will nourish far beyond this moment alone.

Leadership will leave you with wounds. Some of them will become scars. But scars are not something to hide; they are something to point to. They tell the story of mistakes made, storms weathered, and lessons learned the hard way. Will there be personal cuts and bruises along the way? Yes. But there comes a moment when you no longer need the bandages. Healing has already taken place.

And once the bandages come off, you have demonstrated to others that survival and growth are possible. Then, this insight becomes contagious.

Most people see contagiousness as a negative concept. I see it as multiplication. Imagine if great leadership were contagious, easily spreadable to others. Imagine people lined up, simply hoping to catch that leadership itch, hoping to learn how to serve, endure, and lead with integrity.

With my whole heart, I believe we can inspire movements like this.

But it is up to us to forge the path. So let me ask you this: What's stopping you from becoming the best leader you can be? Is there anything in your way, preventing you from preparing the best meal possible with the finest ingredients? What holds you back from becoming the mentor someone else is praying for?

The answers to these questions are less about sourcing failure and more about seeing opportunity for greater impact.

Curious about your impact? Try this. Review the growth of your mentees. Leadership is not about what you can do well. It is also revealed by those we nurtured well. Take a moment to reflect on who took what you taught, grew, and are leading on their own. You planted the seeds. Now is the time to see the harvest.

Let me leave you with one final encouragement: Never just fit in. You were not called to blend; you were called to stand out. That is how you become outstanding. Technical skills may get you in the door, but durable skills keep you there. And in seasons of pain, remember that those who are rejected today are often respected tomorrow.

Lastly, I want to close the way my mother always did. She used to tell me, "I don't have money to give you, but what I have for you is prayer." My prayer for you is that through this book, you find at least one truth to carry forward, one principle to apply, one ingredient to enhance your leadership. My goal is for you to embody this not just at work, but in your home. If that happens, then this meal was worth preparing.

In each season, even if the meal is finished, remember the work is not. What you prepare next will depend on the ingredients you choose, the care you give, and the heart you bring into the kitchen. Don't just fill plates. Feed people. Don't just manage kitchens. Protect the purpose of them. Don't just use ingredients. Honor them.

Lead with intention.
Season with wisdom.
Serve with humility.

And when it's finally your turn to step away from the table, may it continue to nourish people long after you are gone!

Appendixes

Appendix A:
The THANKFUL Method at a Glance

The **THANKFUL Method** was not created in theory. It was formed through years of leadership, observation, failure, prayer, and refinement. This framework is designed to translate across organizations, industries, families, and communities because leadership at its core is relational, not positional.

T - Transparent — Leads with honesty, clarity, and consistency. Speaks truth without hidden agendas.

H - Humble — Understands that authority does not equal superiority. Let's work and character speak.

A - Adaptable — Reads the room, adjusts with wisdom, and responds without abandoning values.

N - Nurturer — Develops people intentionally. Invests time, patience, and care.

K - Kneeler — Leads from prayer, not pride. Seeks guidance beyond self.

F - Faithful

Remains steady through difficulty.
Loyal to purpose, family, and calling.

U - Unifier

Builds bridges during tension.
Protects culture and community.

L - Loyal

Earns trust through action,
consistency, and protection of
the mission.

Appendix B:
Leadership Self-Assessment
(THANKFUL Inventory)

Use this assessment to identify growth areas. Rate yourself honestly from 1 (Needs Growth) to 5 (Consistent Strength).

______ Transparency
______ Humility
______ Adaptability
______ Nurturing
______ Prayer and Faith Alignment
______ Faithfulness
______ Unity Building
______ Loyalty to People and Purpose

Reflection Prompt:

- Which area surprised you the most?
- Which area requires immediate attention?

Appendix C:
Hiring Discernment Checklist
(Chapter 6 Reference)

Before you "go shopping," ask:

- Does this person align with our values or just our needs?
- Are we hiring for relief or long-term impact?
- Have we prayed over this decision?
- Does this person strengthen or strain the culture?
- Will this ingredient improve the entire meal?

If you cannot confidently answer these questions, keep shopping.

Appendix D: Mentorship Readiness Guide (Chapter 5 Reference)

Before agreeing to mentor someone, reflect:

- Do I have time to be consistent?
- Am I willing to be honest, even when it's uncomfortable?
- Can I carry someone's growth without controlling it?
- Am I mentoring from ego or calling?

Mentorship is not about influence.
It is about stewardship.

Appendix E:
Leadership Warning Signs
(Chapters 4, 7, and 8 Reference)

Pay attention when you notice:

- Emotional exhaustion without reflection
- Increased comparison or jealousy
- Neglect of family or spiritual disciplines
- Avoidance of difficult conversations
- Desire for visibility over impact

These are not failures.
They are indicators of a need for realignment.

Appendix F:
Home-First Leadership Framework
(Chapter 8 Reference)

If leadership is strong at work but weak at home, the foundation is cracked.

Ask yourself:

- Does my family receive my best or my leftovers?
- Am I present or just physically available?
- What ingredient is missing in my leadership at home?

Strong leaders protect their home kitchen first.

Appendix G:
Setting the Table Exercise
(Chapter 9 Reference)

List your current leadership table:

- Who is seated correctly?
- Who needs repositioning?
- Who does not belong at this table?

Leadership is not exclusion.
It is alignment.

**Appendix H:
Reflection on Legacy
(Chapter 10 Reference)**

Answer honestly:

- What did my leadership leave behind?
- Who grew because I stayed faithful?
- What taste will remain when I am no longer in the room?

Legacy is not built at the podium.
It is built at the table.

The THANKFUL Leadership Assessment

THE THANKFUL LEADERSHIP ASSESSMENT

A Personal Leadership Posture Evaluation

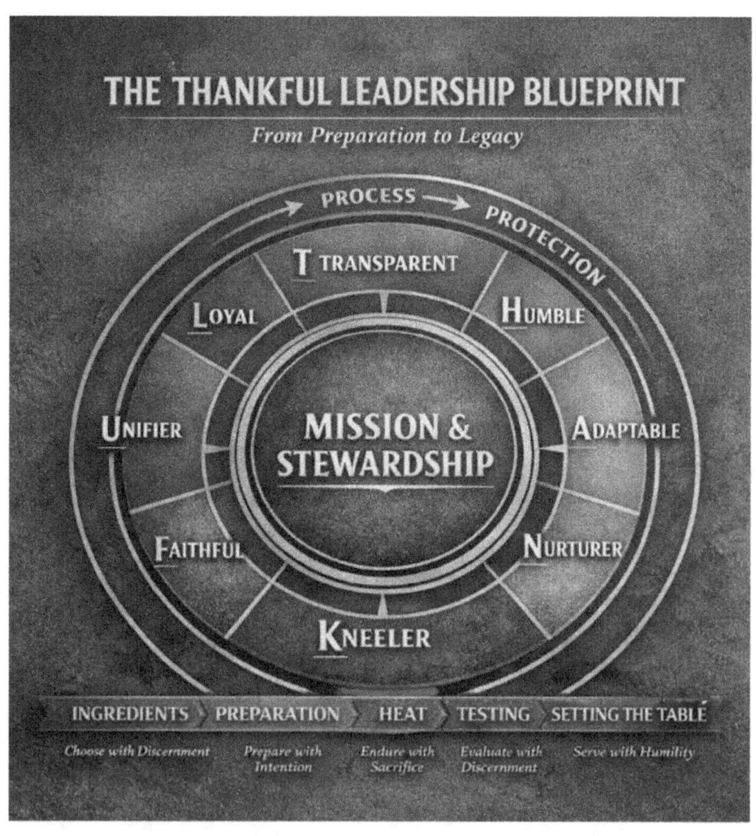

INNER RING

Mission & Stewardship

Before evaluating ingredients, evaluate your center.

1. I see leadership as stewardship, not status.
2. I prioritize people over personal recognition.
3. I make decisions with long-term impact in mind.
4. I consider how my leadership affects families, not just outcomes.
5. I regularly reflect on the legacy I am building.

Subtotal (Mission & Stewardship): ______ / 25

THE 8 INGREDIENTS

T – Transparent

1. I am honest about failures, not just successes.
2. I do not hide behind my title.
3. I address issues directly rather than indirectly.
4. My team feels safe bringing concerns to me.
5. I communicate clearly when expectations shift.

Subtotal: ______ / 25

H – Humble

1.   I listen more than I speak in important
        conversations.
2.   I admit when I am wrong.
3.   I actively seek feedback.
4.   I celebrate others without comparison.
5.   I do not need credit to feel secure.

Subtotal: _______ / 25

A – Adaptable

1.   I respond thoughtfully rather than react emotionally.
2.   I adjust strategy without compromising values.
3.   I remain steady during change.
4.   I welcome new ideas even when they challenge mine.
5.   I can pivot without losing trust.

Subtotal: _______ / 25

N – Nurturer

1.   I intentionally develop others.
2.   I know the goals of those I lead.
3.   I follow up consistently.
4.   I am patient with growth.
5.   People feel seen, not used.

Subtotal: _______ / 25

K – Kneeler

1.   I pause before making major decisions.
2.   I seek wisdom beyond my own experience.
3.   I do not allow ego to drive my leadership.
4.   I reflect before responding under pressure.
5.   My leadership is grounded, not impulsive.

Subtotal: _______ / 25

F – Faithful

1.   I keep commitments.
2.   I show up consistently even when tired.
3.   I do not abandon responsibilities when they become inconvenient.
4.   I remain steady through difficulty.
5.   I finish what I start.

Subtotal: _______ / 25

U – Unifier

1.   I address tension early.
2.   I refuse to participate in gossip.
3.   I build bridges across differences.
4.   I protect team culture intentionally.
5.   I correct division with courage and care.

Subtotal: _______ / 25

L – Loyal

1.   I protect confidential conversations.
2.   I speak well of others when they are absent.
3.   I do not leverage relationships for personal gain.
4.   I defend the mission, even when unseen.
5.   My team trusts my motives.

Subtotal: ______ / 25

OUTER RING

Process, Protection, Multiplication

1.   I am patient with growth.
2.   I guard culture intentionally.
3.   I mentor someone consistently.
4.   I measure success by who grows, not just what grows.
5.   I prepare others to succeed beyond me.

Subtotal: ______ / 25

TOTAL SCORE

Add your score from all ten sections.
Maximum Score: 250

Your Score: ______ / 250

INTERPRETING YOUR RESULTS

225-250

You are leading with strong alignment. Stay intentional. Guard against complacency.

190-224

Healthy foundation, but some ingredients need strengthening. Identify your lowest two sections and focus there.

150-189

Inconsistent posture. Growth is required before expansion. Strengthen character before scaling influence.

Below 150

This may be a season to recalibrate. Seek mentorship. Slow down. Rebuild from the center outward.

REFLECTION QUESTIONS

1. Which ingredient scored lowest? Why?

2. Where might jealousy, ego, or fatigue be influencing your leadership?

3. Who is experiencing the effects of your weakest ingredient?

4. What one habit can you change this month?

5. Who can hold you accountable?

FINAL REMINDER

Leadership is not measured by titles.
It is measured by taste.

If people leave your table nourished, you are leading well.

If they leave depleted, something in the recipe must change.

Stay in the kitchen.
Protect the ingredients.
Set the table with intention.

Dr. Andy Oguntola is a distinguished leader, father, husband, mentor, and advocate for purpose-driven leadership, with a career spanning over 17 years in higher education, organizational leadership, and community initiatives. He is widely recognized for his ability to develop people, cultivate thriving cultures, and build sustainable frameworks that empower leaders and organizations to multiply their impact.

As the creator of the **THANKFUL Method**, Dr. Oguntola has distilled his lived experiences, mentorship, prayer, and discernment into a practical, actionable framework that guides leaders to lead with character, humility, and purpose. His approach emphasizes stewardship over status, service over self-interest, and legacy over recognition, principles he has both practiced and tested in real-world leadership challenges.

Beyond his professional achievements, Dr. Oguntola is a devoted husband and father, grounding his leadership philosophy in family, faith, and community. He believes that true leadership begins at home and is refined through responsibility, reflection, and intentional action.

Through storytelling, actionable insights, and thought-provoking reflection, Dr. Oguntola inspires leaders to bring their best ingredients to every table, whether in the boardroom, classroom, church, or community. Readers and audiences alike are challenged not only to lead effectively but to leave a lasting impact that multiplies through others.

www.ingramcontent.com/pod-product-compliance
Lightning Source LLC
Chambersburg PA
CBHW051519030726
47592CB00006B/2348